'Ben Lindsay's book is a must-read for the
punchy and deeply honest about the issue of racism in the UK today
and in the UK Church. This book is shaped deeply by the gospel
call for transformation: of individuals, of communities, of society at
large. It is my prayer that we heed this call and respond together to
the mandate to challenge discrimination in all its forms.'
Justin Welby, Archbishop of Canterbury

'Too often Christians have assumed that being colour-blind is the
best way to approach race and ethnicity in the Church. Ben Lindsay's
compelling book opens our eyes to this naivety and challenges us
to be willing to have a more serious conversation. At this critical
moment in our national life, when race, immigration and the UK's
relationship with the world is being negotiated, this important and
timely book needs to be read, discussed and acted on.'
Dr Krish Kandiah, Founding Director of Home for Good and author of *God Is Stranger*

'It is most refreshing to read a book with this title and to recognize
that, at the heart of it all, it is about God's mission and the need for
the Church to engage with this in order to fulfil its mission. Ben
Lindsay skilfully weaves in the impact of the human stories and
challenges "all" the Church, not just with what they are reading but
also with the searching questions set at the end of each chapter for
discussion. He reflects on the reality that the active presence of black
people in worship does not translate into leadership representation
and he quotes the Bishop of Rochester who said, "it is, in my view,
undeniable that there is racism within the system, because gifted
people have not found their way into senior leadership." He draws
on the Acts of the Apostles as an example of diverse leadership in
action, reflecting the people of God (Acts 13.1). Ben is not afraid to
highlight the "blatant bias towards white leadership and the stereotyping from the white majority church culture." Black congregations

are also challenged about how they concede to white leadership over black leadership and Ben addresses the issue of tokenism trumping deliberate and intentional development of black leaders and the expectation for the latter to "adapt, assimilate and conform to white ideals." This book should be read by all in senior leadership in the Church and those involved in theological education. Until this issue is addressed head on and young black people are able to see visible images of themselves in senior leadership within the Church, the Church's mission will be seriously damaged and impeded. I will be telling lots of people about this book as it is more than an excellent read – it is geared for action.'

The Reverend Prebendary Rose Hudson-Wilkin, Chaplain to the Speaker of the House of Commons

'Thoughtful and well considered, Ben Lindsay tackles the space where race, religion and culture intersect in a book that is at once both insightful and relatable.'

Chimene Suleyman, contributor, *The Good Immigrant*, co-editor and contributor, *The Good Immigrant USA*

'Ben Lindsay says we need to talk about race, and he's right. Through an impressive synthesis of Scripture, history, literature, pop culture, sociology and personal narrative, Ben invites us to have a much-needed conversation and gives us a host of resources to help us. Provocative, frank and often challenging, this is also a pastoral and very human book, with insights to consider on virtually every page. Come and see.'

Andrew Wilson, Teaching Pastor, King's Church London

'I found myself getting excited during the reading of this book, for Ben is a rarity. In his book he tackles some of the difficult issues that relate to race, such as white privilege and colour-blindness. Through the careful use of life stories, Ben highlights the perennial challenges faced by people of colour in predominately white churches and suggests possible ways in which such ongoing negative experiences can be addressed by the Church.'

In light of Brexit being a critique of both the presence and contribution of people of colour in the UK, this book provides an opportune challenge. It is a gracious and robust reminder that on the matter of structural and institutional racism, the Church is found wanting. The reader is first implored to listen to the injustice that hangs in the collective psyche of the Church and, second, to do something about it.

If you are a white church leader seeking to develop a multicultural church – an authentic, inclusive church that enables the thriving of all people, not just some – then this is a must-read book. It is not a comfortable read, which I applaud. Ben calls out racism, but does not present simplistic, sophisticated strategies as a way of dealing with the root causes of racial injustice in church culture. Rather, he suggests that getting to know the 'other' calls for relationship building, which can often be messy and complex, but is worth it.

This is an excellent book. I recommend all church leaders seeking to create an authentic multicultural church to read and discuss the book's content with their church. If churches can read this book with the openness it calls for, it can, over time, become a game changer for so many churches engaged in the complex world of building a "church for all nations."'

Wale Hudson Roberts, Baptist Union of Great Britain›s first Racial Justice Coordinator

'Every year something happens that makes race an issue for institutions and wider society. On a daily basis something happens that makes race an issue for individuals of colour. The Church needs to look under the surface to really understand what the deep-seated issues around race are, including a Eurocentric view of the Bible, rather than exploring the issues of race in the Bible, as well as the context in which it was written.

Ben Lindsay's book reminds us, and also challenges us, to keep the conversation open about individual experiences, fears and deep concerns, I believe the Church has come a long way, but it has much further to go in terms of the issues of race. This book will help in that process.'
The Revd Les Isaac, Co-founder of Street Pastors

'This is one of the most important books to have been written in recent years and is essential reading for every Christian and especially every church leader in the UK. We can hope that racism no longer impacts life in the UK and particularly our Church, but in this book, Ben Lindsay highlights the ways in which this goliath remains alive and well, and ripe for the slaying. Rejecting false notions of "post-racialism" and the naivety of "colour-blindness", he lays the question of inclusion at the doors of churches in the UK and asks, "How will you respond?" Ben puts on speakerphone the voices of people of colour that are often whispered or silent and invites us to listen. This book is an invitation for the white majority to enter into the discomfort, even pain, that many people of colour experience as minorities among them. It is an invitation first to repentance and then to reconciliation, so that we may love one another more faithfully and, by our love, show ourselves to be disciples of Jesus.'
Selina Stone, lecturer in political theology, St Mellitus College

'Ben Lindsay challenges Christians racialized as white to consider the legacies of white privilege in the contemporary Church. Serious engagement with the contents of the book demand radical action in the composition of leadership, persistent Christian anti-racist practice and exorcism of the demon of "colour-blindness".'
Robert Beckford, Professor of theology, Canterbury Christ Church University

'Delivered with a perfect balance of truth and grace, this book will open the eyes of many. As a young black man navigating in a predominantly white world, this book is a timely weapon of wisdom and a game-changer.'
Guvna B, rap artist and author of *Unpopular Culture*

'Even at a time when racial discourse is very much mainstream and we think we've heard it all, Ben Lindsay's book is a fascinating eye-opener around history and representation in the Church. What I liked most was that, at a time when the voices of the marginalized are rising up to share their experiences like never before, Ben Lindsay shines a light on the struggle with being a black Christian and being black in a white majority church, handling it with sensitivity, fact and practical strategies to bring churches into the modern-day conversation.

Having grown up attending Sunday school and Scripture classes, much of Ben's writing cleared a fog for me that I had internally questioned, but never voiced as a child. Ben sensitively explains that, while the Bible may talk about racial diversity and unity, in the UK today, diversity is a start, but inclusion is the ultimate goal.

The book is a gripping journey through the lens of race and religion and underlines why churches must take a proactive stance and start conversations about opportunities that make religion more inclusive. It includes questions about self-awareness, equipping both the religious and non-religious with an understanding around the Church and its complicated racial history. A must read.'
Jasmine Dotiwala, Head of Youth Engagement, Media Trust

'Meeting Ben Lindsay was like meeting my own story, as he began to articulate one of the most significant topics in the twenty-first century: being black in a cross-cultural Church. I am a black British-born man and not only does Ben articulate the subject that is so personal to me, he is also fearless and faces it head on in this book by stating the obvious issues around race, colour and matters that are big in the wider Church. His questions really do require answers from within the Church in the UK. Thank you, Ben, for being that voice which speaks and challenges our twenty-first-century thinking around culture, colour, race and church.'

Noel Robinson, musician and worship leader

'The book is honest, unapologetic and has integrity. Linking yesterday, today and tomorrow, this book is awake to the issues that perpetuate the structures, systems and human capital that uphold racial inequality within the Church in the UK. It offers a way for healing and thus inclusivity through taking action in truth, reparation and reconciliation.'

Dr Elizabeth Henry, National Adviser Minority Ethnic Anglican Concerns

Ben Lindsay is founder of the charity Power The Fight (www.powerthefight.org.uk), which trains and empowers communities to end youth violence. He is also a pastor at Emmanuel Church London. One of the *Evening Standard's* Progress 1,000 London's most influential people for 2018, Ben is an experienced speaker, trainer and facilitator with more than 18 years working with high-risk young people in the field of gangs and serious youth violence. *We Need to Talk about Race* is his first book.

Follow Ben @bcwlindsay
Follow Power the Fight @PowerTheFightUK

WE NEED TO TALK ABOUT RACE

Understanding the black
experience in white
majority churches

BEN LINDSAY

First published in Great Britain in 2019

Society for Promoting Christian Knowledge

36 Causton Street

London SW1P 4ST

www.spck.org.uk

British Library Cataloguing-in-Publication Data
A catalogue record for this book is available from the British Library

ISBN 978–0–281–08017–5
eBook ISBN 978–0–281–08018–2

1 3 5 7 9 10 8 6 4 2

Typeset by Manila Typesetting Company
First printed in Great Britain by Jellyfish Print Solutions
Subsequently digitally reprinted in Great Britain

eBook by Manila Typesetting Company

Produced on paper from sustainable forests

For H, E and R
May our ceiling be your floor.
Love,
Daddy

CONTENTS

ACKNOW-
LEDGEMENTS

I would like to thank Emmanuel Church London for allowing me the space and time to complete this book. Your prayers, encouragement and support have been felt. Thank you.

Thank you to Woolwich Central Baptist Church for nurturing me in my childhood. Forever grateful. Also thanks to King's Church London for your discipleship and your continued love.

To all the contributors and people I've interviewed – Stuart Baker, Steve Chalke, the Revd Dr Kate Coleman, Nana Guar, Dr Elizabeth Henry, The Revd Les Isaac, Jahaziel, Eleasah Phoenix Lewis, Dr Pauline Muir, Vivienne Neufville, Noel Robinson, Steve Tibbert and Andrew Wilson – thank you for your time and honesty.

Thanks to Juliet Trickey and all at SPCK for the opportunity to write this book.

Special thanks to Michael and Erika Barry, Hannah Bourazza, Samuel J. Butt, Simone Clarke, Madeleine Davies, Jonathan Downing, Ede Ebohon, Rachael Glass, Owen Hylton, Stu and Livy Gibbs, Josh and Katie Greenway, Guvna B, Andrez Harriott, Alan Higgins, Anthony and Temesa Hurren, Emmanuel Imuere, Alwin Kamara, Sean Macnamara, Joe Macnamara, Steve and Lynne Mathews, Claude Murray, Tristan Newman, Wale and Eerika Omiyale, Anika Peterkin, Laura Price, Ben Rowe, Jason Shields, Paul and Massy Spencer, Clare Stell, Selina Stone, Dominic Toms, Phil and Sarah Varley and Rebekah Walker for your prayers, encouragement and wisdom.

Mum, thank you for never putting limits on what I can achieve. Thank you for your endless support and introducing me to the love of Jesus. You truly showed me what sacrifice and perseverance means. Thank you for always being there. I am who I've become because of your prayers. You're the best and I love you. Dad, thanks for your consistent reassurance during this process.

To B, your love, trust, patience, wisdom, insight, honesty and understanding helped me to complete this book. In the dark times you were light. You're a blessing. You are the heartbeat of our family. Thanks for being part of this journey. I love you and appreciate you.

To the Most High, King of Kings, our Lord Jesus Christ. Thank you for the power to write this book. You initiated this – I just obeyed. Thank you for holding on to me in the dark moments. Thank you for saving me. Forever yours. Continue to guard my heart. All praise and honour goes to you.

This book is dedicated to the memories of Emmanuel Odenewu, Nicolas Pearton, Shaklius Townsend and Myron Yarde.

For the culture.

For God shows no partiality

ROMANS 2.11

INTRODUCTION

I CARRIED THIS FOR YEARS

'The most difficult thing to get people to do is to accept the obvious.'[1]
Dick Gregory
African-American comedian and civil rights activist

Being black in a white majority church can be a bit like the first day of a new school on repeat. Your natural insecurities come to the surface. Will I be included? Will I be noticed? How do I connect with the popular people? How do I fit in? Will my contributions be valued? Conversations feel like hard work and at times even painful without the ease of shared histories and friendship.

As a minority you experience verbal and non-verbal slights and indignities on a regular basis that, although brief and commonplace, can lead to a deep feeling of isolation and exclusion. I was at a Christian conference a few years ago when a white church leader commented on my high top/Afro hairstyle asking, 'Is that a basketball thing?' Perhaps he was genuinely curious, but the highlighting of my difference and the implied assumptions surrounding the question – that all black men are into basketball (even though I don't play basketball) – made me feel uncomfortable. Was I being oversensitive or was his comment racist?

This kind of encounter, known in psychology circles as a 'racial micro aggression', is a constant occurrence in the life of a black person. Comments like these often come from well-intentioned white people, but without space to examine our racial biases and discuss misconceptions and misunderstandings, you can see how easily hostility can arise. Often in church, this hostility is hidden from view, but that doesn't mean it isn't there. Many people of colour struggle to feel integrated and included in white majority churches. Whether it's the lack of representation in church senior leadership structures or the feeling of exclusion from day-to-day church life, isolation is a theme I hear painfully frequently. A black woman who attended the church I pastor in south-east London said this:

> Too often minority groups have shied away from expressing the reality of their experiences because they do not want to come across as victims. They do not want to be defined by those

experiences and they tire of defending themselves to majority groups who accuse them of self-indulgent navel gazing, and question whether their views, experiences or struggles are real.

With experiences like these, it is unsurprising that statistics show the fastest-growing denominations in the UK are black African churches. The Pentecostal movement has seen an 11 per cent increase in membership between 2012 and 2017, while overseas national churches, such as Chinese, Polish and Romanian churches, are also growing at a phenomenal rate.[2] Are ethnic minorities tired of trying to integrate into the multi-ethnic church the Bible describes, when this seemingly appears to not be a reality? Has diversity become just a value on a church website without any consideration for how the ethnic minority cultures are included within church life?

I've called this book *We Need to Talk about Race* because I believe it is time to have a conversation about race in the UK Church. In this book I explore the complex issues involved in explaining the black experience in white-led or white majority churches. Diversity and integration are important to me. I'm married to a white woman and I have mixed race children. I'm fortunate to have been brought up in a diverse area of the UK. I pastor a church in one of the most diverse boroughs of London. I have a diverse friendship group. My family has always welcomed people from different backgrounds. And yet I have experienced the type of racism that is life threatening and I have experienced more subtle racist micro aggressions too.

At the heart of Jesus' teaching is a message of equality and reconciliation. Though there have been moments when the Church has been at the forefront of social progress (the role of Christians in the abolition movement, for example), the Church must also confront its own complicity in the building of racial structures that still exist today. The Eurocentric presentation of Christianity, which betrays its Middle Eastern/African origins, and the use of Scripture to justify brutal historic acts have created barriers to the faith for some black people in the present day. These are some of the reasons why I am committed to the idea of racial inclusion and unity in the Church and in wider society. This is the reason I look to Jesus, who smashed the dividing wall of hostility so humankind can be reconciled to God and one another. This is why I agree with what Dr Martin Luther King Jr said:

> I definitely think the Christian Church should be integrated, and any church that stands against integration and that has a segregated body is standing against the Spirit and the teachings of Jesus Christ, and it fails to be a true witness.[3]

Talking about race isn't easy. Some of the barriers I have faced in talking to white people about race are defensiveness and dismissiveness. Many of the white people I talk to are not actively racist. They do, however, often struggle to acknowledge the privileges that come with their whiteness or perhaps have simply never considered them. Privileges such as not worrying about what to wear because you're not going to be racially profiled by the police or be a victim of mistaken identity. Privileges like not seeing your physical presence as a constant threat to women, who automatically cross the road or hold tight to their handbags on approach. Privileges like not having to overcompensate when finding positive images of your race in books, films and art for your children because of the lack of representation in mainstream media. Privileges like being able to discover your family history and legacy with ease. Privileges like seeing people who look like you in the highest employment and leadership positions. I could go on.

As Reni Eddo-Lodge puts it:

> White privilege is an absence of the consequences of racism, an absence of structural discrimination, an absence of your race being viewed as a problem first and foremost, an absence of 'less

likely to succeed because of my race'. It is an absence of funny looks directed at you because you're believed to be in the wrong place, an absence of cultural expectations, an absence of violence enacted on your ancestors because of the colour of their skin, an absence of a lifetime of subtle marginalisation and othering – exclusion from the narrative of being human.[4]

This book is not meant to produce white guilt or a 'them and us' mentality. Instead, I want to start a conversation; to create opportunities for prayerful self-reflection, enquiry, understanding and resolution. Ultimately, a conversation that will provoke large and small actions – from black and white people – to help dismantle racist structures in the Church and beyond.

I would like to make a few comments before you delve into this book. I have deliberately focused on the black experience in the UK Church because . . . I'm black. I have grown up in churches where I have been the minority culture. I also pastor a white majority church. This is what I know. While I do not profess to be a spokesperson for every church-going black person in a white majority setting, I know that many people will relate to my experiences. I also appreciate that there are many other forms of discrimination that urgently need to be spoken about. I look forward to reading about the experiences of others as new contributions are made to the topic of diversity and inclusion.

You will notice that I have used the terms black and people/person of colour interchangeably throughout the book. While I'm not happy with the term people of colour, as it still places whiteness at the centre of the discourse (thereby reinforcing the idea that white equals neutral/normal), there are some experiences I describe that are not exclusive to people of African or Caribbean heritage. Therefore 'people of colour' feels the best way to describe these shared experiences of systemic racism. I have also occasionally used the term BAME (black, Asian and minority ethnic) when presenting and analysing data, to be consistent with data-collection methods in the UK. At the end of each chapter there are questions that I hope you will find helpful as you consider and discuss issues of race in your context. These questions are addressed specifically to black and white church members, white church leaders and anyone considering Christianity. I am also aware of black church leaders who lead in a white majority church setting. While there may be shared experiences, these questions are primarily focused on the situation of black people within a white majority context.

In my grappling with Christianity, the UK Church and racism, I have experienced a range of emotions, but I do remain hopeful. I am reminded of the words of black theologian and pioneer of Christianity, Augustine of Hippo:

> Hope has two beautiful daughters; their names are anger and courage. Anger that things are the way they are, and courage to see that they do not remain as they are.[5]

Christians should be both angry about racial discrimination, particularly in the UK Church, and courageous in wanting to change the situation. I'm hopeful that the UK Church can truly represent the glorious picture painted in Revelation 7.9, where 'every nation, from all tribes and peoples and languages' will worship Jesus. For that to happen, the UK Church will need to examine itself; it will need 'to move into the river of the black experience'.[6] We need to open the discussion and start talking about the black experience within a church context. The Church has been silent for too long on the issue of racism. We need to talk about race.

1. IS IT BECAUSE I'M BLACK?

BEING BLACK IN THE UK

'The harsh reality is race, ethnicity, religion, gender, disability status and related categories all continue to determine the life chances and wellbeing of people in Britain in ways that are unacceptable and in many cases unlawful.'

Professor Tendayi Achiume

UN's special rapporteur on contemporary forms of racism, racial discrimination, xenophobia and related intolerance, May 2018

At the age of 14, I had a rude awakening to adulthood. It was a cold January Saturday afternoon and I had just finished playing football for my school team. I was running late for my second match of the day for my Boys Brigade team at Woolwich Common, south-east London. My mum suggested that I get a cab. The cab driver was an older white man, maybe in his late fifties. I sat in the passenger seat. We drove to the top of the road and turned right. As we went down the hill, another car was driving towards us. The gap was very tight for the approaching car to get through, so the cab driver paused to allow the car to pass. The oncoming car, at speed, misjudged the space and crashed into the cab. Slightly dazed, I saw two white men in their twenties rushing out of the car with purpose. I thought they were coming to see if we were all right. Instead, one of the men opened the driver's door and started punching the cabbie, while the other man dragged me out of the passenger side of the car and started hitting me. They kept calling me 'nigger' while repeatedly pummelling my head on to the bonnet of the car. Suddenly it was two against one. I remember screaming, 'it wasn't me' and 'it was an accident' as the blows continued to shower down on me. Eventually I managed to slip out of my coat, leaving my football kit and belongings in the cab. Powered by fear and adrenalin, I sprinted back to my house. I remember my front door opening to my mum with me in a state of complete hysteria. I had been a victim of a racist attack in south-east London.

Three months later, the black teenager Stephen Lawrence[2] was killed in a racist attack a mile away from where the assault on me had taken place. My assault happened on a busy road with lots of people watching. Not one person came to my aid. No one intervened. People were watching a 14-year-old boy being beaten to a pulp. The police never found the attackers. I remember my dad putting up posters asking for information and then the next day seeing them torn up on the pavement. While there was sympathy and letters of concern, support and encouragement from individuals from my local church about the incident, I do not recall the church calling for a prayer or community meeting to address the issue of racism that was having such an impact on black Londoners at that time. I do not remember the pastor of my church publicly denouncing racism from the pulpit. Reflecting back, I'm not sure how equipped my local church was to be a voice for justice and equality for the local community.

The sad truth is, ask any black person, rich or poor, young or old, who was living in south-east London in the early 1990s, and many will have a similar story to share. As black people, our parents teach us that education is the key to a successful life but, as American writer Ta-Nehisi Coates puts it, 'Some black people will always be twice as good. But they generally find the white predation to be thrice as fast.'[3] This was certainly the case for my black friends and me in the 1990s.

Level playing field?

In 2018, the BBC published a report on career progression and culture for its BAME staff. The aim of the report was to identify gaps and best practice. It found that BAME employees were under-represented in senior positions. As a result, the organization committed itself to establishing leadership programmes and pathways for BAME employees and measures to evaluate ethnic minority leadership progress.[4] In a blog post written for *Premier Christianity* responding to the BBC's diversity measures, Canon J John wrote:

> The focus of PC/PD (politically correct/positive discrimination) culture is negative rather than positive. It seems to encourage people to see themselves as victims needing compensation rather than those who should strive against the obstacles to make it to the top. It emphasises what has been done to us, not what we should do for ourselves.[5]

J John's call to 'strive against the obstacles to make it to the top', while admirable in theory, makes the common mistake of assuming that people from every culture and race start at the same position. It also assumes that when white people flourish, it is on merit alone, without the benefit of mentors, champions, intergenerational wealth and other advantages. Black people in the UK face all kinds of challenges that white people have probably never even thought about. If you are a white person, the black people you know may never have mentioned these matters to you. It's easy to assume that we all just need to work harder, but what if the UK is not a level playing field for black people? What if it is easier for white people to thrive, right across the class system? Of course, working-class black people share many of the same experiences and challenges as the white working class, but with the additional barrier of race discrimination. Race and class are very much interwoven. It is impossible to separate the two in discussions about structural inequalities. In fact, evidence suggests the 'existing race inequalities are compounded rather than erased by class inequalities'.[6] So for the majority of black people in this country who come from working-class backgrounds, there are many challenges to overcome.

The year 2018 was significant for race relations in the UK. In a strange coincidence, the UK marked three milestones, the first being the seventieth anniversary of the arrival of the *Empire Windrush* at Tilbury Docks, where Caribbean members of the Commonwealth were invited by the UK's government to help rebuild the country after the Second World War. The second milestone was the fact that it was 50 years since the MP Enoch Powell's vile 'river's of blood' political anathema of a hate speech towards black people in the UK. Finally, 2018 marked 25 years since the racist murder of Stephen Lawrence.

Each of these events has in some way contributed to the collective experience of black people living in the UK: the good, the bad and the very ugly of Britain. The hope and optimism black people such as my grandparents felt coming to the UK was met with a barrage of hate from some white people. Whether that came from the police, politicians or the average white person on the street, black people struggled to be seen as equals. Getting good jobs, renting and buying homes and being treated fairly were all a struggle. Even so, many black families in the UK persevered, worked hard and, in most cases, made a better life for their families than they would other-wise have done. I for one will always be indebted to my grandparents for deciding to risk it all and leave Jamaica to start a new life in the UK. While the majority of the members of my family are university educated, have good careers and own their own homes, this is not a given for all black families in the UK.

In August 2017, the UK's then prime minister, Theresa May, announced the 'Race disparity audit', which was launched with a view to publishing data held by the Government to shine a light on how people of different ethnicities are treated across public services. What was discovered was bleak but unsurprising news for black people in the UK.[7] The findings present a clear disparity between white and black people in the UK. In terms of poverty and living standards, the research showed that one in five children in black households were in persistent poverty compared to one in ten white British households.[8] In fact, in nearly every category, from housing to school exclusion rates, from police 'stop and search' tactics to employment, black people, particularly of Caribbean origin, were at the bottom.[9] Acknowledging these difficulties and disparities does not mean that I am playing the race card or creating a victim mentality – I'm just presenting the facts.

We can be fooled into thinking of racism as simply superficial and surface-level verbal abuse. The truth is, racism is structural and often unseen, its purpose to consolidate power for the majority culture while blocking ethnic minority cultures from flourishing. There is evidence to suggest that even the most well-educated and affluent black people in the UK face race discrimination (I encourage you to read *Brit(ish): On race, identity and belonging* by Afua Hirsch for more on this). Clearly being middle class does not make you immune. As black academic Kehinde Andrews says, 'The unfortunate truth is that it is delusional to pretend that racism can be overcome by amassing more qualifications. Much wider shifts in society are necessary to ensure equality for all.'[10]

In 2009, the University of Bristol published a study looking at the racial bias in teachers' marking. The 'Test scores, subjective assessment and stereotyping of ethnic minorities' study exploited the typical way that teachers marked examination results, known as 'non-blind', 'to compare differences in these assessment methods between white and ethnic minority pupils'.[11] Looking at all state school pupils in England, the results were that, on average, black Caribbean and black African pupils are under-assessed relative to white pupils. In other words, based on the teachers' 'local experience of an ethnic group'[12] the classic way of marking affected the assessment of black pupils in the education system. Racial bias influences how teachers mark work, so right at the start of black children's educational journies, they are already facing discrimination.

The portrayal of black people in the media is also detrimental. For example, the European Commission against Racism and Intolerance (ECRI) has highlighted the nationalistic, anti-immigrant propaganda by parts of the UK press as 'contributing to creating an atmosphere of hostility and rejection'.[13] UK politicians have been neglectful and ill informed in terms of their opinions of black people. For instance, when talking about the increase in knife crime in the UK, the media and politicians are quick to blame black people. In 2007, the then prime minister Tony Blair, while speaking in Cardiff on knife crime, said, 'We won't stop this by pretending it isn't young black kids doing it.'[14] While official UK crime statistics acknowledge that knife crime disproportionately takes the lives of young black people in London and other major cities in the UK, these statistics present a skewed view of the nationwide picture. Journalist Gary Younge has pointed out:

If we are talking about 'knife crime in Britain', it cannot be reduced to race and culture in the capital – but very often has been. Half of the children killed by knives in Britain are not in London; of those, only around 15% have been black in the last decade. Indeed, taken as a whole, two-thirds of the young people killed by knives in Britain, including London, are not black.[15]

It is important for white-led and white majority churches to understand the misperceptions, stereotypes, hidden trauma, hurt, struggles and collective pain that some black people are dealing with. The UK has never been a level playing field for black people and if the UK Church becomes conscious of this fact, then we can begin to contextualize our churches so that they can set about meeting the real needs of our communities.

Secondary trauma

On 14 August 2017, I wrote a response on social media to the Unite the Right rally in Charlottesville, Virginia, United States. Organized by the far right, 'its stated goal was to oppose the removal of a statue of (Confederate soldier) Robert E. Lee from Emancipation Park.'[16] During the rally, a man linked to white supremacist groups rammed his car into a crowd of counter-protesters, killing one person and injuring another. President Donald Trump failed to denounce the actions of the far right, saying there was 'hatred, bigotry, and violence on many sides'[17] a comment that was widely condemned and ignited more protests and riots in America. One young black man, 20-year-old Dre Harris, was brutally attacked at the rally. I typed the following Facebook post:

> Still not seeing enough condemnation and outrage about #Charlottesville. Trust me, if you're white, your best black friend knows that this could happen in the UK. The black people at your work and places of worship and at your gym know this

could happen in the UK. Show him or her you care and engage with what's going on. Don't be afraid to talk, ask questions, speak out against racism and show solidarity. #Charlottesville.

The post came out of the continued bombardment of videos and images of black people being killed in the USA. Since 17-year-old, American black teenager Trayvon Martin was killed in 2012 by George Zimmerman, a neighbourhood watch volunteer, social media platforms have been filled with videos and images of black people being murdered by American law enforcement officers. Although I didn't recognize it at the time, as I reflect back I realize that I was suffering from secondary trauma. The National Child Traumatic Stress Network defines secondary traumatic stress as:

> the emotional duress that results when an individual hears about the first-hand trauma experiences of another. Its symptoms mimic those of post-traumatic stress disorder (PTSD). Accordingly, individuals affected by secondary stress may be themselves re-experiencing personal trauma or notice an increase in arousal and avoidance reactions related to the indirect trauma exposure.[18]

Some of the symptoms of secondary trauma include hopelessness, anger, cynicism, sleeplessness and fear. I was suffering from all these things and the more I saw the lack of empathy from white friends, particularly white Christians, the more frustrated I became. There was too much silence and neutrality regarding the situation in Charlottesville. This was distressing, disappointing and shocking to my soul. I wrote more posts on social media to express my feelings. Speaking to other black people, clearly there has been a psychological and spiritual effect that the continued unjust murders have had on the black community. Yet the question remained: if we are all members of Christ's Church and the Bible says, 'If one member suffers, all suffer together' (1 Corinthians 12.26) where was the empathy, compassion and responsiveness towards this particular situation from the part of the body not directly impacted by what was happening? The pain I felt watching men and women who resembled me being executed by people who are meant to protect us was amplified by a largely indifferent Church.

Lack of empathy

When it comes to issues that excessively impact black people, in my experience the Church seems to struggle to know how to engage. I have no doubt that in some cases the heart is there, but words and actions too often seem to be missing. I've often heard white Christians say that they want to participate in conversations on race or social issues that predominantly impact black people, but they are afraid of saying the 'wrong thing'. This is a common and natural reaction. My response is always twofold. First, history tells us that until the majority culture engages with minority culture issues, structural injustices will remain (this happened with slavery and the civil rights movement in America). Second, silence will be interpreted as apathy or collusion. Sitting on the fence when it comes to racism or racial inequality is not an option – action is required. This urgency to act is echoed in the words of Reni Eddo-Lodge:

> If you're disgusted by what you see, and if you feel the fire coursing through your veins, then it's up to you. You don't have to be the leader of a global movement or a household name. It can be as small scale as chipping away at the warped power relations in your workplace. It can be passing on knowledge and skills to those who wouldn't access them otherwise. It can be creative. It can be informal. It can be your job. It doesn't matter what it is, as long as you're doing something.[19]

The more white churchgoers engage with the social issues that excessively affect black people, the more integrated and empathic the Church will become. But how do we achieve this meaning-fully? How can we engage in this complex and, at times, painful conversation?

White supremacy

If we do not acknowledge, recognize and admit that there is a problem, we are never going to find solutions. Very few white people would say that they support white supremacy (the racist ideology based on the belief that white people are superior in many ways to people of other races and, therefore, white people should be dominant over other races). There is no doubt, however, that, historically, the con-cept of white supremacy has been woven into the fabric and structure of our society, which is to the detriment of black people and to the benefit of all white people.[20] Reni Eddo-Lodge states, 'if you're white, your race will almost certainly positively impact your life's trajectory in some way. And you probably won't even notice it'.[21] One of the questions I am frequently asked by white people is, 'What practical things can I do to help?'

Figure 1, overleaf, is my adaption of what is sometimes called 'Acts and omissions'[22] or the 'white supremacy iceberg'. The idea is that most white people are not actively racist (the top part of the dia-gram). The tip of the iceberg is socially unacceptable and, in some cases, illegal. I have, however, heard overtly racist language used in a church context – and this must be confronted, but, more often, it's the second part of the diagram that many white people participate in or contribute to upholding. It is in this second part that real change can occur. Whether a white person is in church, in the office or at a social event, it's what's below the surface that can become second nature and, therefore, can become normalized if left unchallenged. It's this secondary, hidden layer that helps to maintain structural ra-cism. This can take the form of denying that racism exists, denying white privilege, not speaking up where there is clear discrimination in the workplace or staying quiet when racist banter is overheard.

Melting the iceberg

Two white friends recently gave examples of attempting to melt the white supremacy iceberg in their contexts. One, who works in the film industry, challenged an older white man to stop using racist language on set. Another friend, who works for a national newspaper, was part of a conversation about diversity. Most of his colleagues felt that the office *was* diverse. My white friend challenged that

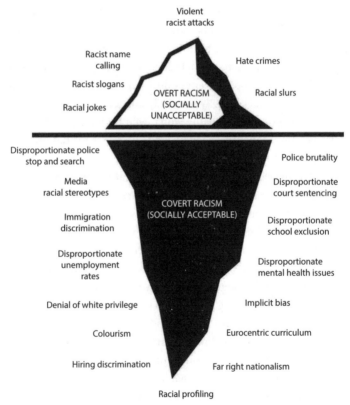

Figure 1 **White supremacy iceberg**

perception by saying that, while there were women, there were hardly any people of colour. As a result, there was a review on diversity at the newspaper. My friend observed that while progress had been made to strengthen gender diversity at the newspaper, the results indicated that greater investment was required in other areas, notably ethnic diversity and ensuring that different needs are understood and accommodated across the business.

While it's yet to be seen if there is any sustained change in the film studio or at the newspaper, these are examples of white people acknowledging inequality and overt/covert racism and saying something about it. They give us helpful models to follow. Silence should not be an option when it comes to racism. Can the white-led, white majority UK Church become more empathetic to the issues that some black people are dealing with?

One pastor famously said that we are to 'walk across the room'[23] to engage with those on the edge of church life. I would take this idea further and say that the UK Church should not just walk across the room but also actively encourage black brothers and sisters to participate in redesigning, decorating, rearranging and shaping the room. Only then will the UK Church gain a better understanding of the black experience and start working towards true ethnic unity in the body of Christ.

For your consideration

Person of colour Are there first-hand experiences of racism or, indeed, symptoms of secondary trauma that may be impacting you? Is there anyone you can speak to?

White church leader If you are serving a racially diverse congregation locally, how aware are you of the societal issues potentially having an impact on your black members?

White church member Revisit the white supremacy iceberg. Are you engaging in racist acts that you were not aware of? Are there areas of your life where you can actively begin to dismantle the overt or covert racial structures around you?

Looking in Have any of the issues of racism mentioned in this chapter impacted you personally and do you think the Church should play a role in addressing them?

2. FAMILY FEUD

RACISM IN THE CHURCH

'Racism doesn't have to be blatant, to be dispiriting, and it doesn't have to be intentional to be real.'[1]
Charlie Brinkhurst Cuff
Consented magazine

My earliest memory of racism was at the age of seven. My family had just moved to our new house in Charlton, south-east London. One evening, we were returning home from my grandmother's house and, as we entered our gate, we noticed shattered glass on our driveway. Someone had thrown a brick through our window. Over the subsequent weeks there was racist graffiti on our home and dog excrement left on our doorstep. Not long after these incidents, my mum realized that members of the far right and fascist political party the National Front lived on our street. Monkey noises and shouts of 'nigger' became a regular occurrence.

My second memory of racism is when my white neighbour's daughter offered me a mouthful of her milk, but not before asking me 'Not to leave any black on the bottle.'

Similar racist incidents continued during my youth, varying from the petty to the life-threatening, but this didn't stop me from making a diverse group of friends. To my mum's credit, she welcomed all races into our home. The main reason for this was her unwavering faith in Jesus. If Jesus welcomed all, so would we. My mum truly demonstrated that Jesus is for everyone through her hospitality. Jesus always played an integral part in our lives. My grandmother was a Christian too and went to a local Baptist church in Woolwich, south-east London. My mum and I went to a different Baptist church in the same area.

This was the 1980s. The area was deprived and council blocks surrounded the church. The congregation was predominantly made up of white working-class families. People were friendly and very welcoming, but I was the only black person in my friendship group. I remember when I was three years old, I returned home from church, looked in the mirror and realized that I was not white, that I was not like all the other children at church. On another occasion, I recall an interaction with a parent of one of the children I was friends with at church who was Scottish. I was ten and he took great pleasure in telling me that my surname – Lindsay (a Scottish name) – was not my own; it had been 'given' to me. Although I did not realize what this older white male was saying at the time, my mum explained that he was informing me my last name would have belonged to my ancestor's slave master. My friend's father had made the point loud and clear – I was not to associate my black self with his proud Scottish heritage. I did not appreciate the history lesson.

Colour-blindness and colour consciousness

As I got older, I found myself conflicted. Through my church family, I had met some of the kindest, most loving, encouraging and generous people. Yet, on occasion, an awkward racial dynamic would cause me to question my place in church. I remember an occasion in the 1980s when my mum had come home from her midweek prayer meeting. There had been a discussion about Nelson Mandela, who at the time was serving life in prison, accused of conspiring to overthrow South Africa's apartheid rule (the system of institutionalized racial segregation and discrimination in South Africa between 1948 and 1991). That evening, a white church member had described Nelson Mandela as a terrorist and said he deserved to be locked up. That was a view shared by the then UK prime minister Margaret Thatcher.[2] My mum, being the dignified women she is, refused to be drawn into an argument with the white church member and let the comment slide. However, I knew my mum was deeply hurt.

Questions reverberated around my head after hearing about this exchange and seeing the frustration on my mum's face. Why did my mum have to ignore the comment? Why couldn't the white person have shown more empathy to the struggle of black people being discriminated against and being killed in South Africa? Why couldn't they appreciate the affinity my mum had with other black people going through that struggle? Where was the support, prayer and encouragement for those suffering in South Africa? Why was this global atrocity not being discussed, prayed about, even preached about in our local church? Isn't God a God of justice as well as grace? Why did no other white person stand up for my mum and, importantly, for Nelson Mandela in that situation? The church lacked the ability to thoughtfully engage with such issues.

One thing I learned from the Mandela incident, and the things I continue to see in churches today, is this: there is a huge difference between churches being diverse and churches being inclusive. Attracting black people to church isn't difficult. For many of us, as black people, church is a major part of our life and heritage. Creating inclusive communities, however, where black people feel that they are a valued part of the culture, not just observers, is more complicated. Sadly, the racism we see in society we also face in the Church, through a combination of ignorance, naivety and white privilege. This is exasperating and painful for black people.

There is a strange colour-blind mentality within the Church (seeing everything as race neutral), which can make the topic even more difficult to raise. Many Christians would argue that God does not see colour so why should we?[3] God loves all people the same, judges all people the same and holds all people to the same holy and moral standards regardless of their skin tone. When Jesus died on the cross, he died for all – without distinction of colour.

While this is all true, we cannot ignore the other end of the spectrum – colour consciousness. We cannot and should not ignore, disregard or overlook how God made each of us individual. As Isaac Adams said:

We love people less when we ignore how God made them. And we are nothing without love (1 Corinthians 13). Jesus was born at a specific time, into a specific culture and given a specific identity. God is all about the detail.[4]

While some Christians will view a colour-blind approach as a positive thing – a demonstration of loving all regardless of race – there is also a danger that if white church members do not have a degree of colour consciousness, they will ignore the realities, concerns, joys and fears people of colour experience. This is imperative because being colour conscious gives white people license to explore and learn about diverse cultures and helps people of colour to feel valued and welcomed in traditionally white spaces. Finally, colour consciousness brings a truer representation of God's value of diversity in the body of Christ, helping to bring a glorious melody of diverse tongues coming from peoples of all nations, all colours, praising him together around the throne in diverse ways.

Although as Christians our absolute identity is in Christ, we are to navigate ways of retaining the consciousness of people's identifiers. Otherwise, misunderstandings happen and opportunities to learn from those with different experiences are missed.

Why be inclusive?

At the heart of Christianity is a desire for unity of humankind under the banner of Jesus Christ. We see God's commitment and promise to Abraham, that through him God would build a unified, diverse body of believers – all nations being blessed (Genesis 12.1–3; 22.15–18). God's yearning to see all, no matter what background or nation, joined to him continues through King David, with the promise that from his bloodline one will come (Jesus) through whom 'all nations will be blessed' (Psalm 72.17). This message of unity continues through the prophets in the Old Testament, where a wonderful picture is painted of a restored and reconciled world in which not only the Jewish people but all nations will worship together (Isaiah 2.2).

In the New Testament, God's promise to Abraham is fulfilled in Jesus Christ. 'Faith in Christ provides full access into membership of the new covenant people of God.'[5] Through the book of Acts we see the good news of Jesus Christ crossing all cultures, ethnicities and nations, as 'the people of God are gathered into local assemblies that proclaim and reflect the glorious gospel of Christ.'[6] The Bible begins and ends with a message of inclusivity. In the final book of the Bible, John is given the ultimate picture of integration:

> After this I looked, and behold, a great multitude that no one could number, from every nation, from all tribes and peoples and languages, standing before the throne and before the Lamb, clothed in white robes, with palm branches in their hands, and crying out with a loud voice, 'Salvation belongs to our God who sits on the throne, and to the Lamb!' (Revelation 7.9–10).

The UK Church would be wise not to view these words as an unobtainable ideal that will only occur once Jesus returns, but instead work and pray diligently to make it become a reality in the present day. Jesus came, died and rose again for all. The quest for racial diversity cannot just be a value on your church website; it must be at the heart of all you do and be something you suffer for. To pursue racial diversity without inclusivity is problematic for the following reasons.

First, it can cause resentment, frustration and isolation for black church members who feel marginalized and misunderstood. Second, racial diversity without inclusivity can lead to passivity, disinterest, integration fatigue or a mentality of fight or flight from the black church member. Third, it can stunt spiritual maturity in black people and limit growth of the church corporately, ultimately becoming a barrier for other black people who may be seeking to join the church.

In differing ways, over time, I've seen all three of these problems play out in my church life. I have seen black people not being integrated into their churches, not being heard, being marginalized, being made to feel like the 'other'. It's worth mentioning that what

I mean by integration is not assimilation, where people leave their culture behind to be accepted into another. Integration means being included in, and creating and contributing to, church culture.

Black skin, white masks?

One of the causes of racial disharmony in churches is 'othering'. This is a term that psychologists use to explain how a person can be made to feel excluded from a group. One of the best definitions I've found of 'othering' is this:

> Any action by which an individual or group becomes mentally classified in somebody's mind as 'not one of us'. It's sometimes easier to dismiss them as being in some way less human, and less worthy of respect and dignity, than we are.[7]

We've all experienced 'othering'. Whether it's your first day at work and no one has invited you out for a work drink or times at school when you've been the last one in the playground to be picked for the football team. But it's especially easy for black people to feel 'othered' in a white majority culture. I have been in church situations where my clothes, physical appearance and music tastes have been high-lighted and white people have set the tone of exclusion, making their norms the benchmark against which everyone else is judged. Sometimes I'm 'othered' in words, sometimes in tone. Black people can be made to feel the odd ones out, not belonging to the 'in crowd'. I was recently at a barbeque where the majority of the guests there were white and a black couple turned up late. Not only were they jibed with the stereotypical 'black people are always late' joke (even though I was there on time) but there was also an expectation that they would bring a stereotypically black dish . . . chicken! Sly jokes were also made about the black man's muscular appearance that, although I'm sure unintentional, played into a stereotype of black male physicality and black body politics.

Whether or not the black couple were aware, they were being 'othered'. How do black people respond to this? As Ta-Nehisi Coates states, we learn to 'code switch and become bilingual'.[8] We save our Nike Air Max and name brand clothes – which some may see as symbols of black urbanity – for when we're out with our black brothers or sisters and reserve our comedy and black conscious talk for people who look like us. A case of black skin, white masks.[9] The situation is best summarized in the song 'Pick up the phone' by the UK artist Ghetts,[10] when he describes how his Jamaican mum speaks three different dialects, depending on who she is talking to – patois, cockney and posh.

What Ghetts describes is typical of a lot of Caribbean parents, but this is also a metaphor for the black experience in general. As black people, we are constantly code switching in ways that white people do not have to, adapting to our environment depending on who the audience is. For some, the pressure is too much to handle. They yield and become 'the mask, while others overcompensate'[11] and turn every perceived offence or violation into warfare.

I recognize that it is human nature to compartmentalize people. We develop biases and stereotypes based on our experiences or the images presented in the mainstream media. People of colour live with the effects of these stereotypes on a daily basis. The feeling of being labelled can be a barrier to building relationships and can have a bearing on a black person's well-being and sense of self. For example, I've found the clothes a black person wears or the car he or she drives have different connotations when viewed through the lens of a white person, which can lead to negative outcomes for that black person. When a white person sees a black man driving an expensive car, like a BMW or a Range Rover, he or she may assume that he is a drug dealer. A white man with the same car would be unlikely to face the same scrutiny. I don't have an expensive car but, as a black man, I often feel that I am fending off negative assumptions about myself before I've even opened my mouth.

The sports clothes I wear for my morning run seem to associate me with criminality, creating a sense of fear for some white people (I often notice white people crossing the road or holding tightly to their bags as I approach). A black friend, who is a GP, tells me that she is often mistaken for the cleaner or is asked if she knows when the doctor will arrive. These three examples position black people as the criminal, the threat and not worthy of having a top profession. Society projects these stereotypes and limitations on to black people but, in church, where God shows no partiality, black people should be able to expect better.

One of the biggest battles for people of colour is to find and then keep our cultural accent – an expression of our cultural heritage. What I've had described to me by men and women of colour in my congregation are versions of the same story: 'I'm exhausted by dealing with racism and discrimination in my workplace, so why would I choose to identify with a church community that shows no more understanding of the issues I face than my white work colleagues?' From their perspectives, maybe attending an all-black church would be easier.

So how do we prevent 'othering'? How can white Christians grow in empathy and wake up to issues that matter to the minority culture? How can churches become inclusive spaces and not just diverse at face value? It is going to require white church leaders and members to work harder at developing an unbiased church culture that truly represents and speaks to the community around them.

Culture

There are many Bible verses that speak about racial diversity and unity. These include, 'Every tribe and language and people and nation' (Revelation 5.10), 'There is neither Jew nor Greek, there is neither slave nor free, there is no male and female, for you are all one in Christ Jesus' (Galatians 3.28), and, 'One new man in Christ.'

(Ephesians 2.15) While these verses are rich and true, there is a danger that we use them as a blanket message to define church culture. What I mean by this is that we quickly take on the idea that we are all the same and so downplay any difference.

The danger in disregarding difference is that we risk creating a dominant, generic Christian monoculture, a one-size-fits-all model, while ignoring the complex tapestry of the community surrounding our local churches. There shouldn't be a prevailing Christian culture dictating church life in diverse environments. Christianity no more equates to whiteness than being British should just be associated with being middle class. The uniqueness of both Christianity's cultural universality and variety is something black theologian Dr Carl Ellis acknowledges:

> Biblical Christianity is, by God's plan, universal in nature; it can take on itself the identity of any culture. We see this universality of the gospel in the book of Acts. The day of Pentecost, when the gospel was preached in every language of the world is clear proof that the Christian gospel is not locked into a particular culture or language. The call of the church was to penetrate every nation, every culture, with the message of salvation that all peoples might submit to God in their ethnicity. So in Christianity, if I do not worship God in my own culture, I am being inconsistent with my faith.[12]

For the UK Church to go from racial diversity to inclusion and to emulate the biblical descriptions in Revelation 5 and 7, we will need to have difficult conversations about inclusivity and the historic dominant culture in the Western Church.

Listen

True racial integration in the UK Church will require white church members to become better listeners to the experiences of black people. Black people are experts in distinguishing between sincerity and artificiality on the topic of race. The important thing for white people here is not to take things personally. If I disclose a racist experience to a white person, that doesn't mean I'm connecting that experience to the white person I'm talking to. Alternatively, some comments from white people will trigger memories of previous racist experiences, so, as a black person, I need to decide whether the white person is coming from a place of malice or ignorance. Some conversations might be clunky and awkward at first, but it is important to remember that not all comments are intended to be racist. Some white people are trying to connect or find common ground and do not realize how their attempts to relate come across (I have lost track of the number of times I have been greeted in church with an awkward 'Yo' or an elaborate handshake, fist bump, high five combination by a white person attempting to be 'down' with black culture).

Conversations about race can be petrifying for a white person. No white person wants to be accused of being racist. Here are some helpful points to consider from a great article by Kesiena Boom entitled '100 ways white people can make life less frustrating for people of colour'. [13]

- Just because you can't see racism around you doesn't mean it's not happening. Trust people of colour's assessment of a situation.
- Don't assume that all people of colour share the same views. We are not a monolith.
- Don't make embarrassing jokes to try and be 'down' with people of colour. We'll laugh *at* you, not *with* you.
- Read books and watch shows by people of colour.
- Have a critical eye when watching TV and movies. How are they portraying people of colour and why? What purpose does it serve?
- Use your white privilege to be on the frontline between people of colour and injustice. You're at much less risk than us.

- Listen when black people say, 'I'm not comfortable in this situation.'
- Understand that nothing in your life has been untouched by your whiteness. Everything you have would have been harder to come by if you had not been born white.

Safe spaces

On launching Emmanuel Church New Cross in a racially diverse area of south-east London, I appreciated that I needed to take my leaders on a journey to better understand the historic and present issues specific to the local context. In July 2017, I read *Why I'm No Longer Talking to White People about Race* by Reni Eddo-Lodge.[14] It is one of the best books I've read on race from a UK perspective, covering issues such as the histories of racism, systematic and structural racism, what white privilege is and race and class. In a bold move, I bought copies for my predominantly white leadership team. This was bold because, for the first time in my life, I was voluntarily opening up discussions about race with white people. As uncomfortable as it was to debate the topic of racism, I realized that if we were going to have a truly racially diverse, inclusive church, everyone needed to be part of the conversation.

Stuart Baker, a white pastor at Emmanuel Church London, shared his experience of reading the book:

We were at a leaders' meeting for our church when Ben handed out the book *Why I'm No Longer Talking to White People about Race*.[15] I remember feeling a bit bemused by the title, as I thought about the sight of me, a white guy in his thirties, reading this on my commute to work in south-east London. As I have thought about it more, the reason that I think the title jarred is that it was defining me by my race, as being white. It's fair to say this is not a typical experience for me. I rarely consider the fact that I am white, and the privileges and advantages that this brings.

This made me think more critically about myself and that's not a bad thing. The biggest myth that the book laid bare for me was that all racism is easy to spot. That racism isn't just the use of fascist language or the noise you used to hear from the BNP, it exists deeply in structures of our society. The challenge for me was that this structural racism exists because members of the dominant white culture, like me, aren't thinking critically enough about the implicit biases and nudges that make my experience as a white guy that much easier than someone who isn't white. I hope that's something I'll get better at doing.

As a Christian, I naturally read the book through the lens of my faith and, as I did so, my mind kept turning to the biblical ideas of justice and reconciliation. I ended up actually feeling hopeful because, while both the Church and I have a long way to go on this issue, as Christians we can be equipped by the truth of who we believe in. The one who is never passive and always opposes injustice.[16]

As pastors in a diverse area, building an integrated multiracial community, we realized that it's important to be aware of, and sensitive to, people's histories and to take action swiftly when issues of race arise in church. Leaders have a responsibility to ensure that majority culture members in the congregation are culturally aware and equipped to demonstrate empathy and understanding to minority cultures. It starts from the top and trickles down. Leaders set the culture.

Reconciliation

My own involvement in church, along with the experiences other black people in primarily white churches have shared with me, revealed that not everyone's past participation in church life is positive – specifically regarding race. Some people have been burned and it makes them understandably tentative. On the launch day of Emmanuel New Cross, Samantha (pseudonym), a young black woman, came to the service looking very nervous. The church was primed to be welcoming and hospitable. She shuffled into the building and sat at the back of the room. Being our launch Sunday, the church was packed and I preached from the heart the vision I felt God had given me for the area. At the end of the service, I went and found Samantha and spoke to her. What she said shocked me.

Samantha	I was very nervous about walking into your church.
Me	Why?
Samantha	There are too many white people here and I have a problem with white people. I have had bad experiences, specifically with white people in a church context.
Me	I'm sorry to hear that. How did you find the service?
Samantha	Before I answer that, due to the number of white people here and because I heard you were married to a white woman, I guessed that you would have no idea about black issues and there was no way I could relate to you.
Me	Right . . . well . . . erm . . . how did you find the service?
Samantha	I was blown away by the welcome and your sermon was on point. It actually made me realize that I have prejudices against white people. Will you help me?

I was undone. In one conversation I saw what our church could be and how far we were from achieving it. Samantha had reminded me about reconciliation. In my mind, there was a combination of what it says in Romans about us being reconciled to God through

Jesus (Romans 5.1–11) and in Matthew about being reconciled to one another where there is conflict (Matthew 18.15). It was at that point I knew the type of church God wanted us to become: a racially diverse, integrated church that is not afraid to discuss issues which have the potential to expose racial disharmony and concerns that may have become barriers for people of colour experiencing Jesus and flourishing in church life.

I was reminded again of the necessity for our church to be open about issues of race at a leader's meeting not long after my conversation with Samantha. As people began to arrive for the meeting, I noticed a white woman greeting a black woman by complimenting her hair. The white woman then proceeded to touch her hair. In my experience, this is a cultural misstep. The black woman and I caught each other's eyes in a way that only black people would understand. I could tell the black woman was upset (even though she continued to act normally). The next day, I texted her and encouraged her to talk it through with the white woman so that no resentment would fester and the white woman could benefit from a cultural lesson. The white woman did indeed gain cultural insight and apologized, and the black woman felt heard and empowered.

What could the landscape of UK churches look like if white majority churches became more empathetic to issues of race, taking swift and deliberate action to reconcile cultural misunderstanding? As JAY-Z might put it, there are no winners when families feud.'[17]

For your consideration

Person of colour Are the examples given of 'othering' experiences that you recognize? Are you confident enough to talk to your church leader about how you feel?

White church leader Reread Stuart's comments about being given Reni Eddo-Lodge's book. Can you relate to anything he said?

To what extent do you prioritize racial inclusion and integration in your church?

White church member Reread Kesiena Boom's statements from her article '100 ways white people can make life less frustrating for people of colour.' Can you remember any times when you may have done things she says you shouldn't? How do they make you feel?

Looking in Is the universality of biblical Christianity something you've ever considered? Does this make you see the Church, and what it could be, differently?

3. WHY BLACK MAN DEY SUFFER

THE CHURCH AND SLAVERY

'One cannot correctly understand the black religious experience without an affirmation of deep faith informed by profound doubt. How can one believe in God in the face of such horrendous suffering as slavery, segregation, and the lynching tree? Under these circumstances, doubt is not denial but an integral part of faith. It keeps faith from being sure of itself. But doubt does not have the final word. The final word is faith giving rise to hope.'[1]
James H. Cone
The Cross and the Lynching Tree

I am unapologetically black and I am unashamedly Christian, yet, if I'm honest, I have struggled to see how these two identities can be compatible. Classic Hollywood movies and TV shows such as *Gone with the Wind*, *12 Years a Slave* and *Roots* always have white 'Christians' owning slaves. This has only reinforced the opinion that Christianity is a 'white man's religion' and a black person's torment. Malcolm X made a fair but damning assessment of the Church saying, 'What is the greatest single reason for this Christian Church's failure? It is its failure to combat racism. It is the old "You sow, you reap" story. The Christian Church sowed racism – blasphemously; now it reaps racism.'[2]

From a young age, I felt the conflict of being black *and* a Christian. Yet, at the age of 22, I discovered the love of Jesus for myself. Nevertheless, I continued to have questions, such as, what role did Christianity actually play in the transatlantic slave trade? Have I been duped into taking on a 'white man's religion' like my descendants before me? Have I fallen for what Karl Marx famously called the 'opium of the people'? These are questions I needed answers to and are also questions not often addressed in sermons in white majority churches.

In my own journey, I wrestled with my own personal experiences as an individual and within church life (touched on in the first two chapters). Since becoming a church leader, I've realized that there is a need to look at a corporate response too. The following chapter will look at the collective and corporate response of the Church to historic racism and how what happened in the past has contributed to our present. Without both black and white Christians sharing an agreed collective memory of past racial wrongs by the Church, it will be difficult to move forwards in unity.

The Church and slavery

When it comes to slavery, speak to any Christian, white or black, and we are likely to fast-forward to the abolitionists and the work they accomplished in ending slavery. These include the eighteenth-century Methodist leader John Wesley (1703–1791); the Anglican MP William Wilberforce (1759–1833), who was one of the main forces in Parliament to end the slave trade in the eighteenth century; James Ramsey (1733–1789) in the Caribbean; and Granville Sharp (1735–1833), who fought for the emancipation of the African Jonathan Strong. While this work is often celebrated, there is another side to the coin – the role Christians played in the slave trade in the first place. The Church's role in the transatlantic slave trade is full of inconsistencies. As Richard Reddie comments, 'Religion was also a driving force during slavery in the Americas. Once they arrived at their new locales the enslaved Africans were subjected to various processes to make them more compliant, and Christianity formed part of this.'[3]

It's the propagation of slavery by the Church that receives minimal scrutiny in comparison to the contribution of the abolitionists. This could be seen as one of the main barriers to Christianity for some people of colour, while adding to the collective amnesia of white-led, white majority churches with regard to the Church's role in the slave trade. The paradox for some black people is this: loving Jesus and understanding his amazing grace is one thing; loving the Church, with its complicated racial history, can be problematic. However, since Jesus loves the Church and died for the Church, the two are interwoven.

Scripture and slavery

The Bible, like other holy books, has been used both to condone and to condemn slavery. As Richard Reddie points out:

Scriptural passages from the Old Testament books of Exodus, Leviticus and Deuteronomy which appear to denounce slavery actually condemn enslavement in certain circumstances rather than slavery in general. On the other hand, although the Apostle Paul's New Testament epistles fail to condemn slavery, they argue that slaves must be treated fairly as 'brethren'.[4]

On arriving in Africa, early European explorers looked to the Bible to find an explanation for the differences in ethnicity and culture they observed, having encountered the already established trans-Saharan slave trade, sanctioned by Islam.[5] They concluded that the enslavement of Africans was a consequence of sin, with Genesis 9.24–27 a key text to hang this belief on:

> When Noah awoke from his wine and knew what his youngest son had done to him, he said, 'Cursed be Canaan; a servant of servants shall he be to his brothers.'

He also said:

> 'Blessed be the LORD, the God of Shem;
> and let Canaan be his servant.
> May God enlarge Japheth, and let him dwell in the tents of Shem,
> and let Canaan be his servant.'

Europeans took these verses and others to justify treating those from a different ethnicity (black people) in the most inhumane ways. First, 'the curse of Ham' gave license to white Europeans to teach that God had created the 'institution of human bondage, and that this arrangement was to be perpetuated through all time'.[6] Second, white Europeans argued that the curse singled out dark-skinned Africans 'for perpetual service to the white race'.[7]

Despite the religious justifications for enslaving Africans, minimal evangelism actually took place in the early days of slavery and, when it did, clergymen were often instructed to avoid the book of Exodus (with its themes of freedom, equality and justice) from their Bible lessons. The conflicts that arose from teaching the liberating message of Christianity to slaves were obvious. The radical inclusivity of the gospel made the inhumane exploitation of fellow believers impossible to defend. As a consequence, the construct of 'whiteness' was used to differentiate between free and enslaved. 'As black men and women claimed Christianity for themselves, "Whiteness" replaced Protestantism as the primary indicator for freedom in the Atlantic world.'[8] This had a direct impact on the practice of Christianity as a religion and the creation of racial categories and hierarchies in the early modern Atlantic world, which favoured whiteness. This European influence from the UK Church provided the foundation of the pro-slavery ideology that would materialize in the late eighteenth and nineteenth centuries.

While the efforts of Quakers such as George Fox (1624–1691) and Benjamin Lay (1682–1759), and Anglicans such as the then bishop of London, Dr Beilby Porteus (1731–1809), are to be celebrated, the UK Church must also acknowledge the crucial and significant role it played in starting the barbaric transatlantic slave trade in the first place. The 'narratives of abolition cannot be reduced to a story of angelic white benefactors gifting freedom to their black wards'.[9]

The 32 images of William Wilberforce in comparison to just 4 images of black abolitionists and anti-slavery activists displayed in the National Portrait Gallery in London tell their own story. It is important to include the efforts of Africans in the UK who petitioned Parliament to end the slave trade. People such as Olaudah Equiano (1745–1797), a former slave who bought his freedom, the abolitionist and autobiographer Mary Prince (1788–c.1833) and Ottobah Cugoano (1757–1791), who wrote the pivotal *Thoughts and Sentiments on the Evil and Wicked Traffic of the Slavery and Commerce of the Human Species.* Cugoano lobbied for swift action to free enslaved Africans in the late eighteenth century, at a time when the UK government was slow to move on ending the slave trade. It is also vital to mention that black people on plantations were already rebelling against their slave owners in the early eighteenth century. Rebels such as the Maroons, who in 1655, escaped from slavery on the island of Jamaica and established free communities in the mountains, where it was difficult for their owners to find them. Other slave uprisings included Barbados in 1816, Demerara (today's Guyana) in 1823 and again in Jamaica in 1831.[10] It was the 1831 rebellion in Jamaica, led by Samuel Sharpe (1804–1831), that insisted on introducing a working wage for all slaves. This rebellion was also one of the main vehicles towards abolition. I can relate to writer Leah Cowan's comments when she says:

> Embracing knowledge that enslaved Jamaicans participated in leading the movement for freedom, and in fact wrestled liberty from the hands of slave owners, rather than it being gifted by white British Christian abolitionists, redefined my understanding of Jamaica . . . I've learnt to accept that 'History' – a knowledge form so dominated by white male narratives – rarely presents a multiplicity of voices, but that a more measured narrative always comes out in the wash.[11]

Direct impact

Life is full of complexities and contradictions and the Church is no different. For every Anglican bishop who stood up against the atrocities of slavery, there were others who were complicit in keeping it going. Many white Christians have used the age-old argument, 'why does the issue of slavery matter now?' or 'the transatlantic slave trade ended long ago'. Speaking to the musician Jahaziel, who in 2015 renounced his Christian faith, he reflected on the damaging impact slavery and colonialism has had on African spirituality, and how it is still found in the Church today:

> My first experience of racism within the Church was in a black church. The pastor had a thing about men having to

wear shirts and ties and to have their hair short. I never thought it was a racism issue, I thought it was a cultural thing, but looking back, I realized it was a colonial mindset. The pastor had been given a certain view of what is proper, what is smart according to a Western standard. I didn't think much of it until I went to a church in Kenya and the pastor was very much the same. [He] was wearing a shirt and tie, and it was really hot and people were singing these Hillsong-type of songs. I went to Kenya hoping to experience the culture and something authentic and what I got was Old Kent Road [London]. This is so saddening, that you have been robbed of your culture and adopted someone else's and you call this holiness, this alien culture you call Christianity and I have a big problem with that.[12]

From Jahaziel's perspective the transatlantic slave trade has left an imperialistic taste in many contemporary expressions of church. The question is how can the UK Church present Jesus out of the shadow of its dark and complicated history? Can a white person who was not born at the time of the transatlantic slave trade be responsible for past atrocities? There are two things to acknowledge here. First, while it's fair to say that black people in the UK are no longer in chains, there is an assumption that past historic events, such as the transatlantic slave trade, have left no apparent scars on subsequent black generations, as if to say the damage caused has no impact on our present. Second, our present culture is extremely individualistic; Christian culture shouldn't be. The Bible talks of God's people as 'we', as the 'body' as a 'nation'. This is our corporate identity. Therefore, there is a collective responsibility for the past wrongs of the community – especially if, in some shape or form, we are still benefiting from or being impacted by those past wrongs.

The UK has and continues to benefit from slavery, whether it's the innovation of the Industrial Revolution, which was a direct result of the wealth generated from the slave trade, or our current banking system, which can trace its roots to financing and insuring slave ships (the Bank of England, Lloyds, HSBC and Barclays to name a few). Even though the slave trade ended in 1833, the UK, through colonialism and neocolonialism still profited from countries impacted by slavery in the first place. From ordinary UK middle-class families to current well-known UK millionaires, there are scores of people who benefited from UK government compensation at the end of the slave trade, through inherited wealth. Even the cousin, six times removed, of former British prime minister David Cameron, General Sir James Duff, in the late 1700s, received £4,101 (the equivalent of £3 million today) in compensation after 202 people he enslaved on his sugar plantation were freed.[13]

The effects of slavery still reverberate in the UK and around the world today. The 18 August 2018 marked the 500-year anniversary of the beginning of the transatlantic slave trade. It marked when the king of Spain, Charles I, began the transportation of slaves direct from Africa to the Americas. When we consider the numbers of Africans directly impacted by the transatlantic slave trade and its multiplying effects, we begin to see the cost and destruction visited on black people. The figures are frightening. Just before the start of the twentieth century, the transatlantic slave trade was responsible for the enslavement of approximately 24 million African men, women and children.[14] The impact of the slave trade on future generations has been catastrophic. European powers had fused some 10,000 African polities into just 40 colonies, often bringing together diverse groups with no collective history, faith or language.[15] Economically, the landscape of the world has changed for ever, as estimates suggest that 40 per cent of Africa's private wealth is held offshore.[16]

If you are looking for more evidence that the impact of slavery affects us today, look at the UK Treasury. In 2018, the department tweeted its 'surprising' #FridayFact:

Did you know? In 1833, Britain used £20 million, 40% of its national budget, to buy freedom for all slaves in the Empire. The amount of money borrowed for the Slavery Abolition Act was so large that it wasn't paid off until 2015. Which means that living British citizens helped pay to end the slave trade.[17]

In other words, along with other UK taxpayers, my grandmother, my parents and I have been paying taxes (the modern equivalent of about £17 billion) to compensate those who enslaved our ancestors. This is a fact that fills me with pain, not pride. I'm reminded of the words of musician Erykah Badu:

> For an African to escape the cruels of inferiority complexes due to colonialism unharmed, is like sucking on a big, thick juicy mango without its nectar slowly dripping down your wrist. You just can't do it without getting physically sticky or psychologically penetrated.[18]

Body politics

It's not just the financial damage slavery has inflicted on black people that should be acknowledged. In Chapter 2, I mentioned my experience of watching a black friend being slyly ridiculed by white people for his muscular appearance. While some may think that I'm being overly 'sensitive' or cannot take a bit of 'banter', this type of stereotypical, generalized and lazy conversation happens all too often to black people. As commented on the blog two: AM in their opinion piece 'Physicality and crafting the black male identity':

> This concept pertaining to black people roughly boils down to the ideology that Black people are bodies not minds. This is a cultural myth that persisted covertly and overtly since slavery. It attempts to negate the systemic oppression the Black

community faces in the educational system, and reinforces the racial hierarchy that we experience today.[19]

Whether consciously or not, some white people place the physicality of black sportspeople over the obvious hours of practice and diligence dedicated to the craft. Tennis player Serena Williams is one such example. She holds the most tennis Grand Slam titles in singles, doubles and mixed doubles combined among active players, yet some people put this all down to the way she is built.[20] Sweeping opinions that black people are only suited to a particular type of sport (such as football, sprinting, long-distance running, boxing) have an historic connotation that can also be traced back to the slave trade – where the physicality of black people took precedence over any other human attribute, such as intelligence. Jon Entine says in his book *Taboo: Why black athletes dominate sports and why we are afraid to talk about it*:

> Even raising the subject of black athletic superiority brings angry rebukes from some quarters. William Rhoden, a distinguished African American columnist with the *New York Times*, derides it as 'foolishness,' a white 'obsession,' and an 'unabashed racial feeding frenzy.' Lurking in the background, suggests Rhoden, are racial stereotypes of black mental and moral inferiority. In this garbled translation, black success in sports is not a compliment, but a proxy for racism – a 'genteel way to say nigger'[21]

The question that should be asked is this: why, when a person of colour dominates a field in a traditionally white space, do white people, particularly traditional white media, feel the need to physically, mentally and emotionally dissect them? This is nothing new: conversations regarding race, intellect and body originated from slavery and continued with various racial eugenics theories and practices (such as advocating improving the genetic composition of the human race through selective breeding). These theories were popular during the early twentieth century (see the story of South African Sarah Baartman, who was 'put in a cage and displayed for the English spectators to look at her body'.)[22] Black bodies and black intellect have always been a source of threat and fascination, as well as things to conquer. Entine continues:

> White fascination with black physicality has been part of a dark undercurrent since the first stirrings of colonialism. In the minds of many, the notion of physical differences is tethered to racist stereotypes of an 'animalistic' black nature and the implication that blacks are somehow intellectually inferior.[23]

Racial body politics is yet another legacy of slavery – a collective memory and corporate understanding that we must own to move forwards.

Solutions

It wasn't until 2006, just ahead of the bicentenary of the Parliamentary Act to end the slave trade, that black British descendants of slaves received an apology from the then prime minister Tony Blair[24] and the then archbishop of Canterbury Rowan Williams. The archbishop told the synod that the Church ought to acknowledge its corporate and ancestral guilt, but neither him nor Blair went as far as considering reparation.[25] 'Reparation' is defined as the action of making amends for a wrong one has done, by providing payment or other assistance to those who have been wronged. So is an apology enough? Can and should the Church do more? An apology, while important, is not justice. But is it fair to talk about reparation in a present context when the slave owner and slave are no longer alive? If neither lives to give and receive reparation, what's the point? So how does the Church deal with historic racism that still impacts society today?

Speaking at the Q Ideas conference on race reparation, the Revd Duke Kwon argues that the Church can and should be engaging in the work of restoring and repairing historical racial hurts that have shaped and characterized the Church in the twenty-first century. He reminds Christians, 'the Church was the moral cement for our structure of racism in our nation' and 'we have not yet fully reckoned with our Christian responsibility for the legacy of racism in our . . . society'.[26]

Kwon argues that, 'true repentance, repairs what was ripped and returns what was ripped off'.[27] He uses Luke 19, where Zacchaeus the tax collector meets Jesus, as the basis for his argument. Zacchaeus is so impacted by this interaction he says:

> 'Behold, Lord, the half of my goods I give to the poor. And if I have defrauded anyone of anything, I restore it fourfold.' And Jesus said to him, 'Today salvation has come to this house, since he also is a son of Abraham. For the Son of Man came to seek and to save the lost' (Luke 19.8–10).

Two things are striking here. First, Zacchaeus realizes that a simple apology is not enough. Pain has been caused and therefore a significant offer of repair, above and beyond what is merited, is required. Second, we see that Jesus is pleased with the act. There is a lesson for the UK Church here about what is required to fully acknowledge, repent of and repair the past sufferings of slavery. In the example of Zacchaeus, one part of the body of Christ had been significantly wronged and exploited. Much like the work of Jesus on the cross, we need more than words and goodwill to see lasting repair and reconciliation. Equally, Kwon is not simply calling for financial payback for past hurts (although he acknowledges that we should not drift too far from 'economic considerations') but also breaks down biblical race reparations in the following four ways.

1 **Changing our vocabulary** The Church is to introduce the language of repair in all our conversations: 'We can no longer talk about racial reconciliation without talking about repentance and let's no longer talk about repentance without talking about repair.'[28] This will require white church leaders and members in diverse settings to look beyond their own understanding and start looking at the Church through the lens of the black experience.

2 **Reckoning with our history** The Church needs to have regular and honest conversations about what happened in its history: 'You can't repair something until you've learnt how you broke it in the first place.'[29] There have to be moments of publicly acknowledging the pain and the complicit racist history in the UK Church. Church leaders need to stand up and be brutally honest about what has been done collectively to black people. This will break down barriers to entering our church spaces for those who are sceptical due to issues of race.

3 **Repentant imagination** Kwon says, 'It's no secret that our black brothers and sisters feel alienated in predominantly white churches. We assume that's a product of personal preference. We have forgotten that this experience of black alienation in the Church is also a product of sinful exercises of power in the past.'[30] Churches should not be afraid to discuss past racial hurts, talk about how this pain impacts the present and discuss how to work towards a better future. There is therefore a challenge here for white-led, white majority churches to have these conversations with black people in their congregations and, together, imagine what their churches would look like if black people were involved in every aspect of decision-making, if black people were working side by side with white people in strategy and the implementation of that strategy. How might these actions change and enrich the preaching, hospitality, worship styles, missional and community endeavours and so on?

4 **Less talk, more action** Kwon advocates for churches to go beyond talk and take 'concrete steps to repair our racially broken ministry structures and relationships'.[31] This includes repairing the Church's view on social and economic issues that plague the black community rather than placing them into a 'political/social action' box. We also need to repair broken leadership structures that 'try to add diversity without subtracting control. We must substitute it with a vision of leadership that joyfully centres on the gifts, the assets of our dear black leaders.'[32]

Earlier I said that the idea of reparations in the context of slavery is complicated by the fact that today neither the slave owners nor the slaves are still alive. This is further complicated by the biblical instruction not to visit the sins of the fathers on the children because everyone is accountable for their own sin (Jeremiah 31.29–30). For Christians, there is clearly a tension between the biblical concept of individual accountability and the Christian obligation to pursue justice. Since the effects of slavery are still felt today (to the benefit of the descendants of slave owners and to the detriment of the descendants of slaves), it cannot be an option to leave events of history in the past. We must, as Kwon says, seek to repair the damage.

Jesus was a carpenter. Most carpenters I know repair broken things or create new things. Jesus did both. The Bible says, 'All this is from God, who through Christ reconciled [repaired] us to himself and gave us the ministry of reconciliation [reparation]' (2 Corinthians 5.18). Jesus also said, 'Behold, I am making all things new' (Revelation 21.5). It is this combination of repairing past hurts and building new relationships that we believe, through Jesus, God has done and is doing with us.

This is the blueprint we should hold on to when we consider the complicated and multifaceted history and relationship between race and the UK Church. A lack of empathy and a continued ignorance regarding race issues becomes a stumbling block towards progress for the UK Church. All believers of Christ, as his representatives, have a responsibility to repair the damage of racism and make all things new. If, individually and collectively, Christians of all ethnicities make a conscious effort to be ministers of reconciliation and repair, I believe our diverse communities will be radically transformed. The true heart of Christianity will shine through.

For your consideration

Person of colour Do you grapple with the conflict between being a person of colour and a Christian? Is it something you've ever thought about?

White church leader Reread the summary of the Revd Duke Kwon's four points on race reparation. Have you fallen into the habit of assuming that racial alienation in your church is simply a product of personal preference, forgetting that it is also a product of the sinful exercises of power in the past? What steps could you take to begin the process of repair and reconciliation?

White church member Were you aware of the UK Church's role in the transatlantic slave trade and its implications for today? Are you aware of the privileges you have inherited as a result of the ideas that initiated and maintained slavery? What is your reaction to the idea of reparation?

Looking in Does the vision of repair and racial reconciliation described give you more hope for the future of the Church than you had before?

4. YOU DON'T SEE US

DISENTANGLING CHRISTIANITY FROM WHITE SUPREMACY

'A people without the knowledge of their past history, origin and culture is like a tree without roots.'[1]

Marcus Garvey

Jamaican political leader

Over the years, I have come to the conclusion that the truth about the role of black people and our part in history has been eradicated, hidden, distorted and misinterpreted – whether that be in the education system or within institutions like the Church. The historical and social forces underlying racism go very deep, and we need to understand them if we are going to uproot them.

The whitewashing of history is far from just a Church issue; it's a societal problem. In a recent newspaper article on education, the writer (a teacher) said:

> Amid the units about the slave trade, abolition and the Civil Rights movement in the US, we forget the Civil Rights movement in the UK, unless teachers choose to include specific case studies. The brutalities and crimes of the British Empire are ignored. Even Winston Churchill, who historians have found believed in racial hierarchies and eugenics, escapes scrutiny beyond his war hero reputation. Students are led to believe racism and discrimination came out of the ether in this country. That adds to the marginalisation many feel, and has a profound impact on students' understanding of racism.[2]

White Jesus?

When you picture the scenes of the Bible, do you think of Africa? Do you picture brown people? Look at any historic church document or Western art and you will find a blonde-haired, blue-eyed Jesus, even though he was born in the Middle East and would have had brown/olive skin.

The reimagining of Jesus as a white man began during the early Middle Ages in Europe. In this context, darkness had strongly negative connotations, which led to theologians at the time choosing to represent biblical figures such as Judas and King Herod in dark hues, while showing Jesus, in contrast, as white.[3] It was when Christian artist Warner Sallman painted the *Head of Jesus* in 1940 that the blonde-haired, blue-eyed Jesus image reached its pinnacle. More than 500 million copies of that painting have been printed.[4]

Growing up, I never saw a non-European version of a biblical event. Hollywood perpetuates this idea (the 2014 film *Exodus: Gods and Kings*, starring two white actors as leads, Christian Bale as Moses and Joel Edgerton as Pharaoh Ramses, is just the tip of the iceberg). The whitewashing of Christian history does not end with the depiction of the characters in the Bible, who are consistently given a Scandinavian image, but also extends to its geography. The exclusion of most of Africa in Bible maps, which usually include all of Italy, is one such example. As Keith Augustus Burton states, 'whether consciously or unconsciously, those who assumed the responsibility to enhance the biblical message with pictorial aids failed to use all of the colours on the pallet.'[5] If we are to see true racial integration, genuine racial reconciliation and flourishing of minority racial cultures in traditional white church spaces, then the UK Church will need to retell the story of Jesus. The love story of God and his people needs to be disentangled from white supremacy.

Before people started categorizing humans by skin colour, the Bible revealed in Scripture that the first human beings were Adam and Eve. No nationality mentioned, no ethnicity discussed – just two humans, male and female, representing humanity. What occurred over time was that Scripture was manipulated, distorted and misused to serve ill intentions and selfish ambitions. As already mentioned in Chapter 3, race is a social construct. The Bible tends to focus on ethnic categories more than race but, when ethnic distinctions are spoken about, they are used as a means of identification and never to encourage ethnic supremacy, bias or prejudice. We see this in Acts 13.1, with the description of Simeon, 'who was called Niger' – that is, a black man ('Niger' meaning black). The distinction between how the Bible explains ethnic differences and what later occurred in history is emphasized by African American pastor Norman Anthony Peart:

> It's when we use these practices to generalize or discriminate against others that it becomes a problem, both in secular and religious contexts. The Bible does not present racial identifiers as indicators of the possession or lack of innate abilities and qualities.[6]

Out of Africa

Unfortunately, people who claimed to be ambassadors of Jesus and the Church have manipulated Scripture to support their own agendas. Scripture has been used to justify some of the most inhumane acts. Misinterpretations have resulted in black people being seen as inferior because of a perceived divine curse, and the misreading of Scripture has led to confusion regarding the role and people of Africa in the Bible. Genesis 10 tells us that Noah had three sons: Shem, Ham and Japheth. The family tree of each son is also chronicled. It is important to state that the Hebrew terms 'ham', 'hōm' and 'hammā' all convey the senses of warmth, heat or being tanned. In other words, the people known to this region, Africa, were likely to have been of a darker complexion than those of the surrounding areas. Part of the issue is how we understand biblical Africa in relation to modern-day Africa. Keith Augustus Burton, in his book *The Blessing of Africa*, explains:

> When used in an historical context, Africa must be understood adjectivally. In fact, the name Africa was only introduced to the region when the Romans gained entrance to the continent after defeating Hannibal's army in the Punic Wars. Even at that time, the term Africa only applied to the newly formed Roman province and to no other territory. At some time toward the

end of the Middle Ages, the name was applied to the entire 'continental' mass of the land on which the original Roman colony was located.[7]

It's difficult to hear the term 'Romans' and not automatically think of modern-day Italy, but it is important to note what historian Martin Meredith tells us – that, 'all of northern Africa eventually fell under Roman control . . . From east to west, by the end of the first century BCE (Before Common Era), Rome's empire reached along the coastal planes for 3000 miles, from Egypt to Morocco'.[8]

It wasn't until the late 1960s, with the rise of black liberation theology in the USA, that new resources dedicated to uncovering what the Bible really says about Africa came to light. Black hermeneutics[9] aims to validate black people and people of African descent to have a greater understanding of their major contributions to social and cultural development, as well as to the biblical story. The professor and author Dr Cain Hope Felder, father of black hermeneutics, made the most significant contribution to the study of the biblical Africa with the influential book *Troubling Biblical Waters*. We can conclude that the story of the Bible contains numerous examples of African involvement which white biblical academia has failed to accept. There appears to be a trend for Eurocentric theologians to reject, discard or diminish the fact that black people played any significant part in the Bible. Africa and black people have not just played a part in biblical history; black people and Africa *are* biblical history.

Africans in the Bible

Knowing that civilization derived from the continent of Africa makes the task of highlighting key Africans in the Bible virtually impossible.[10] It could be argued that everyone in the Bible is of African descent. Such a claim is open to scrutiny, so it's helpful to look at the work of Michael C. Burton, in his book *Deep Roots: The African/black contributions to Christianity*. Burton attempts to highlight key black biblical characters and personalities, acknowledging that 'The Bible is full of colour'. [11] This is important information because if we can see the bias that has existed over several centuries in biblical scholarship towards white Western norms, we can, as Cain Hope Felder argues, 'challenge the Eurocentric mind-set',[12] which has been distorted by slavery and colonialism. This is important not just for black people but also for good biblical scholarship generally. Through study and research, we begin to see that many of the great early scholars and defenders of Christianity, such as Augustine and Tertullian, were of African descent and had dark skin, yet a quick search of Google images or a walk around the National Gallery will show that, throughout Western history, these same figures have been represented as white Europeans. This is why the UK Church must embrace a broader and wider theological perspective than is currently dominant in mainstream academia. Black UK scholars such as Emmanuel Y. Lartey, Anthony G Reddie, Robert Beckford, Kate Coleman, Israel Oluwole Olofinjana, Selina Stone, Elizabeth Henry and Eleasah Phoenix Louis (to name a few) should be required reading, so that diverse perspectives on Christianity are understood.

Some would ask, why does this matter? If we are all made in the image of God and are all one in Christ, as the Bible says, what's the benefit of focusing on race and heritage? I would respond that it matters because whiteness has become the norm and the alarming neglect of the contribution made by black people to Christianity has had detrimental effects. First, the disregard for the true picture of history only perpetuates the widely held view that Christianity is a 'white man's religion', thus becoming a barrier to engagement with the Christian message for some. Second, white people have always had examples of pioneers, forerunners, innovators, discoverers, developers and inventors readily available to them in the mainstream. This bias creates a confidence in white people. Black people do not have the same luxury.

For these reasons, it is fundamentally important, in all walks of life but specifically in the context of Christianity, for an accurate, more expansive picture of history to be presented. Sheryl Sandberg, Chief Operating Officer at Facebook, said, 'We can't become what we can't see.'[13] Black people have to work extra hard to find examples of people of colour to aspire to, learn from and emulate. The black British actor Daniel Kaluuya, who won a BAFTA for his performance in the Oscar-winning film *Get Out* (2017) and starred in the box office-breaking *Black Panther* (2018), commented on the importance of being surrounded by and seeing successful black professionals in his field. Commenting on Ryan Coogler, the black director and writer of *Black Panther* and *Creed* (2015), Kaluuya said, 'It was very important for me to see Ryan Coogler be the director – a guy from Oakland . . . It was important for me to see a man helming the flipping massive ship like that, being himself.'[14]

Clearly, having black representation in the film industry was both a major encouragement and inspiration for Kaluuya. We need to be able to have this same representation widely available within the Church. What's attractive is seeing people like yourself contributing, shaping important things and having a sense of belonging, but we're not there yet. By failing to present the contribution that black people have made to Christianity, the Church has left generations of black British people uninspired and lost. What I have observed is an exodus of black people from Christianity in the search of a faith that better represents who they are. Whether Islam or African spiritualism, Rastafarianism or Black Hebrew Israelites, black people are seeking a better portrayal of the black religious experience. Therefore, if the UK Church really wants to go beyond diversity and move towards inclusion, it must present a more accurate and expansive view of its history that is relevant to everyone.

Old school is true school

Earlier in the chapter I talked about biblical figures. It's also important to credit and recognize the African forerunners who have shaped what we know as Christianity today. What follows is just a snapshot of African scholars and theologians from the origins of Christianity. These include people such as Demetrius, who was bishop of Alexandria in Egypt (180–232 CE), who was pivotal in sending missions to Upper Egypt. The result was that thousands of people from poorer communities heard the good news of Christ and became Christians. Men such as Clement of Athens (150–215 CE), who holds the honour of being Christianity's first systematic theologian,[15] and African theologians such as Origen (185–254 CE), known for writing and authoring over 6,000 books. Origen's best-known and most influential work was the first documented effort at biblical criticism in Christian history.[16] Origen was appointed head of the Catechetical School in Alexandria, Egypt, replacing Clement. Other notables include Didymus the Blind (313–98 CE), who is recognized as being the person who invented a script for the blind[17] as well as writing numerous biblical commentaries and Tertullian (155–230 CE), who founded the Carthaginian theological school in Egypt. Tertullian was credited with introducing the term 'Trinity' into the Christian vocabulary, teaching that the one God is revealed in three persons.[18] Tertullian wasn't just a theologian but also an activist, leading mass uprisings and demonstrations against the Jewish and pagan attacks on the Christian Church. Cyprian (210–58 CE) was an accomplished lawyer and became a professor at the Carthaginian school.

One of the people Cyprian influenced most was Augustine (354–430 CE). Aurelius Augustine eventually became the bishop of Hippo, modern-day Annaba, Algeria. This black African man, 'born in Tagaste, Numidia and reared in Carthage is heralded by Catholics as the pre-eminent theologian of Christianity.'[19] Known for being a defender and challenger of the faith, Augustine is recognized for developing the concept of 'original sin'. Augustine wrote over 700 works, including 93 major works, 263 sermons and 260 letters. They include the seminal works *City of God* and *Confessions*.

I have only given a snapshot of the contributions of African people to early Christianity. Unfortunately, African forerunners of the Christian faith continue to be whitewashed and eradicated from Church history. I believe that one of the main reasons Christianity is unappealing to some black people in the UK is that, throughout history – and today – black people have been consistently unmerited by the Church. This is the same Church that, ironically, came from Africa, was cultivated in African education institutions and produced African theologians. The biggest lie is that the history of black people started in the sixteenth century with slavery. Richard Reddie comments, 'Europeans doubtless refused to acknowledge the relevance of African Christianity as it appeared irreconcilable with the continent's cultural surroundings.'[20]

The UK Church has to be careful not to fall into this deception and must present a truer picture of Christian history, which includes the contribution of black and African people. This may be one of the reasons why black majority churches in the UK are growing at an extraordinary rate while others are in decline. The damage caused by the historical whitewashing of Church history, and the continued lack of effort to correct this, needs to be acknowledged and acted on. How does this work in practice? How do we retell the story of Christianity to reflect a more accurate and global view of history? How do we repair the damage, heal the wounds and promote the unifying message of Jesus in a racially diverse context?

Contextualization

To disentangle Christianity from white supremacy, the UK Church needs to become better at contextualization. Contextualization of the Bible involves an attempt to present the gospel in a culturally relevant way, revealing the unchanging truths of Jesus within the unique and changing contexts of cultures and world views.[21] Contextualization is something every pastor has to wrestle with. How do you communicate the gospel in a relevant way to the dominant culture without being accused of watering down the message of Jesus? This is an issue the Revd Les Isaac, co-founder of Street Pastors, has grappled with. He explained to me:

> I have always asked the question, how do I contextualize the gospel? My context was black liberation theology and how people in the States and South America would take arms. But in the UK, we are in a country that is moving further and further away from God and I come from a tradition where we preached the gospel and taught the word. But then the Bible teaches that the Word became flesh and I have always said to myself, how does it become flesh in the schools, in the pubs, to the old people?[22]

The idea that the Church should spread beyond its building and into the community is one that I share. The Church should not be a static entity, expecting the lost to just flock to it – we must be active and mobile.

Andrew Wilson is the teaching pastor at King's Church London, a 1,500-member black majority church in the diverse area of Lewisham, south-east London, and was previously a pastor in Eastbourne, on the south coast of England. He has written many bestselling books. Andrew is white and has numerous theology degrees. While Eastbourne has 20 per cent ethnic minorities, Lewisham borough has 70 per cent. On the differences between Lewisham and Eastbourne, Andrew comments, 'Lewisham is a long way from Eastbourne. It only takes an hour and a half in the car, but it's a journey from suburban to urban, Leave to Remain, white majority to astonishing diversity.'[23]

Over the last few years I've got to know Andrew and have been impressed and fascinated by how he has adapted to his new hyper-diverse environment, where the congregation he now serves is predominantly black. I asked him how the UK Church – specifically, white evangelical churches – could retell the story of Christianity to reflect a more accurate and global view of history? Andrew made three vitally important points and, though the quote is long, I feel it is important to share it in full:

> First, race is a much bigger issue than I had realized. If you're white, you probably don't see it; if you're a person of colour, you see it all the time. Avoiding the subject can seem like an inclusive, open-minded thing to do – 'I don't see colour' – but it actually avoids addressing the many obstacles, injustices, divisions and problems that remain. Many white people see 'colour-blindness' as a strength. Many people of colour see it as a profound weakness.
>
> Second, my preaching and writing was more (and more needlessly) white than I had realized. Since moving to London, I have preached far more than I used to about slavery and freedom, social and ethnic divisions, the reconciliation of Jew and Gentile, the power of history, the reality of privilege, structural injustice and the like. It's not that those themes weren't in the Bible before; it's that I didn't particularly focus on them. My illustrations and quotations, likewise, were drawn from sources that I would naturally read or watch as a white person. That had to change pretty quickly, as I had to contextualize to a new audience. I needed to tell the story of the Church and the story of the world in a way that was far more globally representative (and historically accurate!).

A few things can help [us do this well].

- Telling the story of Christianity forwards, not backwards. The temptation is to start with us (in my case, British, theologically conservative charismatics) and work back, which inevitably highlights the roles of people like us. We need to start at the beginning, emphasizing both the influence and provenance of the Church fathers (many of whom were African and Asian). The bonus here is that they often speak far more about our questions (spiritual gifts, grace, for example) than we ever realized.

- Reading world history can also help. Schoolkids are taught 'our' history, but if we don't work at broadening our vision, we can end up perpetuating a Eurocentric version of world history without realizing it and, implicitly, marginalize the rest of the world (much of which has a huge part to play in the Church's story). This isn't just about colonial history, by the way – there is a certain type of white person who wants to swing to the opposite extreme and denounce everything that white people have done as irredeemably and uniquely awful, which can end up centring whiteness in a different way – but getting to know the history of China, Egypt, Peru, Persia, Ghana and so on for what they are.
- We need to be engaging with specific moments in the Church's story that cause problems for people. In Lewisham, slavery and colonialism are the most obvious ones, but it might be supercessionism in Hampstead, the Crusades in Brent, Christian Zionism in Tower Hamlets or whatever. If we are going to serve people well, we need to connect Scripture, their history and the story of the Church together in ways that are open about our failures, express context as well as regret, and honour Jesus.[24]

It is encouraging that white theologians like Andrew are exploring and actively presenting a more diverse biblical narrative. Likewise, Christians will need to re-examine the stance of some of the most popular and influential biblical scholars. Whether it's theologians with Donald Trumpesque views on immigration[25] or others dismissing repentance and reparation for past racial injustices towards black people,[26] we have to acknowledge that these views are harmful and help to maintain racist structures in the Church. For real structural systematic change to occur, Christians will need to read more broadly, listen to more varied voices and challenge overtly racist theological viewpoints.

Steve Tibbert, who is white and leads King's Church London where Andrew is teaching pastor, demonstrates a commitment and intentionality to the issue of diversity and contextualization:

We did things like diversity training, we got experts in and we were just trying to learn. One of the surveys we did showed that if King's is 1,500 (people attending) on a Sunday, we found out that 900 had joined in the last 5 years; of those people, 70–80 per cent were black Caribbean/black African; and 1,000 out of 1,500 had never heard us teach on diversity and never experienced the diversity course we did in 2008 called *Gracism* (based on Dr David Anderson's book of the same name).[27] There are a lot of people at King's with a Pentecostal background and we are coming from a slightly different place, so we thought we would do a teaching series called *Invited*. It was great. Former director of the Evangelical Alliance, Joel Edwards, spoke and said it was the most intentional teaching series he had ever seen in church on this issue. I was so encouraged. We did it in our midweek groups for seven weeks. We have institutionalized the issue of diversity in the sense that we speak on the topic once a year, normally around Easter. We kept it in the teaching annually and even in the recasting of our vision, diversity is high.[28]

Just as Steve is bringing contextualization into his teaching, Noel Robinson, a black international worship leader, is seeing increased diversity within the area of worship music. Noel comments:

In this era of worship, we are seeing a change in people's expressions. There has been a morphing. There has been a merge, a new baby born called multicultural worship. There are a few of us worship leaders who have the ability to speak several worship languages. We can speak in CCM (Contemporary Christian Music), Pop and Gospel. God is raising up people with a dual culture who are able to flip between both worlds. I see worship in the UK beginning to break the existing model and structures of what people see and what people are used to with worship music.[29]

These examples, from Les, Andrew, Steve and Noel, show that true racial integration and inclusion, as opposed to superficial multi-ethnic attendance, requires a deeper awareness of the past and present racial issues of our congregations and the courage and boldness to tackle the elephants in the room. Let's hope, pray and work for more purposeful acts of reconciliation and inclusivity across the UK Church. Only then will we reverse the damage that the whitewashing of history has caused to the UK Church.

For your consideration

Person of colour Have you noticed a tendency for sermons to only quote white men or use illustrations that pertain to white majority culture? Is this something you could challenge?

White church leader Reread Andrew Wilson's observations on speaking in a black majority context. What could you do to become more informed about the major contributions made by African and Asian forerunners to Christian scholarship? How could their voices be more present in your telling of Christianity?

White church member Have you noticed a tendency for sermons to only quote white men or use illustrations that pertain to white majority culture? Is this something you could challenge?

Looking in Does picturing the events of the Bible through an African lens change your view of Christianity?

INTERLUDE

DON'T TOUCH MY HAIR

'Black women have had to develop a larger vision of our society than perhaps any other group. They have had to understand white men, white women, and black men. And they have had to understand themselves. When black women win victories, it is a boost for virtually every segment of society.'[1]
Angela Davis
American political activist

Through observations and conversations I've had, it has become clear that the intersection of being a woman, black and a Christian is a hard road to travel. If there is an invisible demographic, a group of people who are most likely to be on the edge of church life, who are almost certain to be ignored for leadership and not given the opportunity to shape church culture in a multi-ethnic church, it's black women. In my experience as a pastor, black women are also the people who are least likely to publicly complain about the obvious inequality and discrimination they face. Discrimination such as the lack of leadership opportunities made available to them, only being considered for particular serving roles (worship or welcome team), being excluded from white friendship groups and assumptions that black women only want to associate with other black women.

As a black pastor who pastors a predominantly white church, a good portion of my pastoral time is meeting, listening to, encouraging and empathizing with black women in the congregation. Honestly, sometimes I think I'm trying to convince myself more than the black women I pastor that the type of church I lead is right for them.

Whether articulated or insinuated, black women are seen by some white people as too complicated to understand and too complicated to fully engage with. Speaking on BBC Radio 4, black journalist Marverine Cole said:

> We're strong, we're independent, we're sassy, we're sexy, no nonsense, we're passionate, we're angry, we're aggressive – society really does label us with all of these . . . What's really terrifying is that there are a lot of black women out there who are able to wear this strong impenetrable blazing mask of power, anger and everything and underneath we're crying.[2]

If black women are less likely to be in leadership in traditional white church settings, and can also struggle to integrate into church life, what should be done to change this situation? One female vicar, the Revd Anne Stevens, said:

> We urgently need to put clear equality and diversity policies in place at every level of the Church's life, and then set up a pattern of regular audits to monitor progress and ensure significant improvement. This is about gospel as well as law, as the continuing presence of discrimination in the Church is now significantly damaging the Church's mission.[3]

I want to use this book as a platform to foreground black women's voices. Therefore what follows in this interlude are perspectives and experiences from a range of black women in white majority churches. Some names have been changed at their request.

Temi

Most of the black and Asian women I have met in white majority churches have been raised up as disciples and leaders by churches of their own ethnic groups. I am one of them and I never saw my gender or ethnicity as an issue in terms of leadership, until I entered white Christian spaces. Suddenly, it became rare for me to see women who were leaders in their own right and black or Asian women as leaders at all. Single women seemed to have disappeared altogether or were overworked 'serving'; married women stood holding babies, smiling politely or maybe saying 'just a few words' while their husbands held the microphone; and black and Asian women were only ever on welcome or singing backing vocals. This was a total shock and so disheartening to encounter. White couples are the power holders in these spaces and being a black man with a white wife seems to be the second-best thing, which leaves black women in the cold twice over. In my experience, white majority churches fail to develop women disciples and leaders of all backgrounds, and especially single women and women of colour.

For the many single black women in these spaces, the stereotypes of black women compound this problem. We are characterized as having an attitude or being aggressive if we do not make a special effort to prove that we are not what you think, by smiling at all times, speaking so softly you can barely hear us and not making eye contact (some sarcasm included). This then makes it impossible for us to be mentored by white male leaders, who see us as unknowns on both fronts and fear either meeting a Grace Jones or a Beyoncé. Unfortunately for us, these men are often the most experienced in these spaces and they are often the least able to connect with us.

Women of colour are incredible leaders, but, often, white churches are the bastions of white male leaders and/or white wives and the systems, culture and structures are set up by and for those kinds of people. This inevitably means women and people of colour have extra barriers to overcome to enter and remain in those spaces, and if you are a *woman* of colour, that is multiplied. Frankly, most of us are tired of doing that work – we didn't come to church to jump hurdles.[4]

Jennifer

Colour was never a consideration when trying to engage with others or make friends until I got to this church. I was only really welcomed by Sarah [not her real name]. This may or may not have been a coincidence, but Sarah was not white. She encouraged me to try to forge my own relationships rather than rely on others to make me feel welcome. I vividly remember one instance when I tried to engage in conversation with a group of white women in church. They were polite but not entirely welcoming. I asked what they were doing after church and was told that they were going to a local pub for lunch. I felt rejected as they walked away. Having always been a fairly popular person, I felt that this reaction was somehow my fault.

From that point on, I stuck to spending time with Sarah. I also made friends with Patricia [not her real name], another black woman from church. When Sarah left the church, I felt alone, but I took her advice and organized lunches so I could make friends. All but one of the attendees was black and they ended up being my main friendship group. At the time, I did not attribute this to colour (that the black people felt more comfortable spending time together). I just thought this group of people happened to be the people I had made a connection with.

There are a number of observations I have made during my time at this church. First, we have all found a way of existing in the same space, but the divisions are clear when you observe where each group sits at church and who people interact with during the breaks and after church. I think that one of the reasons for this is that you have a church of different tribes that are unable or unwilling to connect, such as white families and single black parents. This makes it difficult to create a community.[5]

Nana

I've been to my fair share of different churches over the years – Episcopalian (white majority), a few Nigerian churches, an Anglican church (mixed), a traditional black American church and a few non-denominational churches, all white majority. I share this context for two reasons. First, my perspective is not based on any one church in particular. It reflects my experiences over the years. And second, my experience of white majority churches is relative to my experience of more diverse or black majority churches.

Obviously, no two churches are the same; there are cultural and stylistic differences. However, in general, I've observed that where black majority churches readily speak on issues that affect the community, such as youth violence, unemployment, financial struggles, many of the white majority churches I've attended will speak more broadly on issues of 'the human condition', often neglecting to acknowledge the disproportionate struggles that minorities face. So as a black Christian woman, twice a minority, this sets the stage for my experience in white majority churches.

While I don't expect a treatise on social justice from the pulpit every Sunday, here is how a typical service at a white majority church usually plays out for me. Enter church. Exchange pleasantries. Praise and worship comes next, followed by a non-controversial preach. Closing prayer. Wishes for a lovely week ahead as we part ways. Smile-greet-preach-part-repeat. It's all very polite and inoffensive.

And while there is nothing wrong with this routine, as a black woman, it leaves me with an underlying feeling of neglect that I've become accustomed to. Unfortunately, it's no different from what I experience outside of church – and church should be different from the world. There are serious issues black women contend with that affect our sense of identity, agency and well-being, which are not recognized by the church.

I really want to be able to lay my burdens down at church; I can't. For one thing, I don't want to be responsible for shattering that pleasant routine we have going. More critically, there simply isn't the space, the time or the interest expressed in the broader church agenda. At church, I want my realities as a black woman to be acknowledged and addressed. I want to feel valued; I want to feel supported; I want practical advice on battling the institutional prejudices I face every day. But I know this is uncomfortable territory for church leadership. To be fair, I have recently observed greater attempts at discourse about 'inclusivity' and 'embracing diversity' in white majority churches. Unfortunately, the message often comes across as an exhortation to be colour-blind or colour neutral, which isn't very helpful to a person of colour. It's the idea that, in the body of Christ, we're all one and the same on this heaven-bound journey, so let's just be kind and embrace each other's differences. Except, we're not the same and embracing my 'difference' doesn't really help me.

To be clear, I'm not asking for special treatment because I am a black woman. However, I've come to understand that the way the world views me – my skin, my hair, my body, my capacity to think, my ability to lead, my humanity – is different from the way the world views everyone else who is not a black woman. And if a church is to be relevant and supportive to me as a black woman, then it must acknowledge this uncomfortable truth. Then it must create a seat at the table for the black woman's voice. I'd like to see white majority churches actively show willingness to understand this and create spaces to have constructive conversations with black women about their experiences.[6]

Eleasah

I'm half white and my skin is very fair, and I've often felt like I'm the accessible one. In most churches, I always get a yes. While there are many pastors and leaders that value my contribution, I have always had to consider if it was partly because they see me as approachable. I've been to churches where darker-skinned women have tried to stir up the same conversation within their congregation to no avail – so I had to ask myself, why? I wonder if I just tick the box when it comes to churches representing black people. The positions I've held have been different from my darker-skinned friends and this could be purely to do with personality types or perhaps there's a confidence there that I've been afforded in the wider societal/relational context that has helped me to access certain roles in church. I do believe that darker-skinned women are perceived as more aggressive, irrational and angry in our society and that people more readily close their ears and hearts to them. I genuinely want to see the Church's heart change towards black people, African cultures/histories and the rest, but the types of situations I have alluded to do make me question my place. I do believe there are times when I have access to certain social/relational privileges that my [darker-skinned] sisters do not.

To be honest, I've yet to witness the backlash from the black community about it all, but I'm aware that there will be times when I'm going to have to keep my mouth closed and step aside, in the same way I would tell white people to sometimes keep their mouths closed to allow black people's voices to be heard and to speak for themselves.

In terms of being in a black church, in Caribbean churches, I always felt accepted, but it was different in the African churches – I felt like the white girl – but we do have different cultures, philosophies of self and community and historical journeys. It's interesting to see how it all comes to a head in the UK where we're all 'black' and often in the wider social gaze the differences and nuances get lost. Sometimes white people will say openly racist things to me or make suggestive remarks about 'those types of people' and I think, why do you think you can have this conversation with me? Am I like 'black on tap'? With certain white people in my social/professional spheres, I'm only black when they want me to be.

However, when I studied at theological college, I felt like we were speaking about two different worlds and that was largely because the institution did not seem open to my understanding of God – rooted in black and Pentecostal perspectives it didn't seem welcome at the table. I often felt like black Pentecostal Christians were the butt of theological humour. When I would bring questions to the class conversation, I was often shut down or the lecturers would rephrase my questions as if not to offend anyone else in the class. I felt 'othered' – it was actually my awakening to the conversation of race and Christianity. Often in this upper middle-class institution I felt like a handbag or an accessory. – shhh! Don't talk too much. [7]

Vivienne

I have attended several churches over the years and at times find it very sad and frustrating to see that many churches do not always practice what they preach. I have heard a lot of preaching and prayers asking God for a multicultural church, but I sometimes wonder if we really want or expect our prayers to be answered, as this brings people from all walks of life with different traditions, languages, cultures, accents, different styles of worship and praying. I wonder if we are ready, because I have heard it said that we clap too loud and that we pray for too long. I have seen eyebrows raised, music being played out loud in order to drown out the voice of the person who is praying. Because of this we hold back on the way in which we worship, not praying or just saying a few words and not expressing ourselves as the spirit leads. To fit in and not stand out, we change the way we worship (expressive), saying 'Amen' under our breath quietly, stop bringing words of knowledge or in some instances I have known people to even leave the church because it is too controlled or restrictive.

I find that the church is more welcoming to mixed couples than it is when a black couple comes in and this should not be as we are all equal in the eyes of the Lord. Depending on the church we are in, being black, we are less likely to be used in leading worship or to preach, even when you can clearly see that someone is gifted in this area. If you look around in the church, you will notice the divide – the black people are in one group, the whites in another and only a very small proportion mixed with each other. This does not demonstrate the church of Christ.

We cannot want a multicultural church yet expect everyone to look white, speak the Queen's English and worship in the same way. Sometimes [the issue] is not about being a minority in a white church – we can still be treated the same way in an all-black church. If we want to see the church advance, we need to break down cultural and racial barriers. We must imitate Jesus and truly embrace everyone, no matter what colour they are, as we are all made in the image of the Father. It has taken me a while, but I am now beginning to worship as the spirit leads, as I seek to praise my Lord and not man, as it's all about him (my Lord and Saviour). I pray we put aside our differences and love each other as Christ loves the church.[8]

5. LOVE LIKE THIS

RACIAL SOLIDARITY IN THE CHURCH

'The problem is that society is being lied to. Racism is based on a lie. God created one race, one blood. That's the human race. The very idea of the gospel is that we would be one. The world would know that we are Christians because of our oneness, and because of our love.'[1]
John M. Perkins

One nation?

The band Faithless said it first with their song 'God Is a DJ'. The idea that there is one baseline, one rhythm that can bring all people together in unison like a (good) DJ does, is very much the heart of the Bible. Christ is for everyone. Everyone is welcome in the kingdom. Jesus died for all. Our father shows no partiality and neither should the Church. There seems to be a fine line that the Church should tread between understanding we are one race ('Then God said, "Let us make man in our image, after our likeness"' (Genesis 1.26), 'Have we not all one Father? Has not one God created us?' (Malachi 2.10)) and appreciating, celebrating and acknowledging our differences. Too much either way in our theology on race creates an imbalance in our identity as Christians. We are one body with many parts and one picture with many colours. Elevating our togetherness over our differences can result in ignoring the specific issues related to a particular people group. Equally, raising our individuality over our collective identity as Christians can result in tribalism, subcultures and division. We have to acknowledge that race is a construct. It is often said by white evangelicals that black Christians should be cautious in putting their blackness before their identity as Christians. There is truth in this, but the fact is, we live in a racialized society. We have to recognize the impact of this if we are to have any hope of dismantling these racial structures. John M. Perkins, in his book *One Race, One Blood*, comments:

> Race as we know it today is mostly a social theory that was devised and refined over the centuries to serve the economic and religious goals of the majority culture, first in European territory, then later in America. Whiteness, it turns out, is a very recent idea in the grand scheme of history, but it's a powerful one that was used to create categories and systems that would

place value, economically and otherwise, on skin colour and groups of people who were either blessed or burdened by it.[2]

Even if we acknowledge that the concept of race is an artificial device, we cannot deny the lasting impression and power it has had on black and white people today.

Hope

Fortunately the Bible does not shy away from discussing and addressing issues of racial prejudice and contains numerous examples of how we are to work through our differences and find commonality in Christ. Jesus constantly challenged prejudice and inequality. Whether racial injustice (Luke 10.30–37), class prejudice (Luke 17.11–19; 18.22) or gender discrimination (John 4.1–42), in Jesus Christ we have the perfect example of how to challenge intolerance.

The Apostle Paul in the book of Ephesians says Jesus will 'unite all things in him, things in heaven and on earth' (Ephesians 1.10). This is an important message to hear. Even though we can see pain, suffering, discontent and hostility all around us, Paul is reminding us that God is committed to unifying all things for our good and his glory. This gives me great confidence. Regardless of how imperfect and painful a person of colour's experience can be in a white majority church setting, there will be a day when Jesus will bring harmony. This does not mean, however, that the UK Church is to remain static or passive while waiting for the glorious future of peace and accord depicted in the Bible. The Church must be active now to demonstrate its inclusivity or we are falling short of the vision Jesus has for the Church. The majority culture in the UK Church must demonstrate radical solidarity with people of colour. Dr Martin Luther King Jr, in his 1967 'beyond Vietnam' speech, used the phrase the 'fierce urgency of now' to communicate a message of love and inclusion:

This call for a world-wide fellowship that lifts neighbourly concern beyond one's tribe, race, class and nation is in reality a call for an all-embracing and unconditional love for all men . . . When I speak of love I am not speaking of some sentimental and weak response. I am speaking of that force which all of the great religions have seen as the supreme unifying principle of life. Love is somehow the key that unlocks the door, which leads to ultimate reality . . . we are now faced with the fact that tomorrow is today. We are confronted with the fierce urgency of now. In this unfolding conundrum of life and history there is such a thing as being too late.[3]

While King was speaking about the wider fight for civil rights within America, and the necessity for action over sentiment, the same principles apply within the Church. King ultimately presents a picture of the love of Jesus. A picture of love that is radical, urgent, active, strong, bold and deliberate. King paints a picture of integration that requires a robust examination of how we treat one another. Jesus requires his Church, his followers, to imitate him. Jesus stepped off his throne, where he was worshipped and adored and came to a place where he was despised. Jesus came into the discomfort of this world in an act of radical solidarity. The question for the white majority churches in the UK is this: is there 'a fierce urgency of now' to do the same for your black brothers and sisters? Is there a desire to express radical solidarity with the minority culture?

Confessions, repentance and forgiveness

I can relate to Edward Gilbreath in his book, *Reconciliation Blues* when he says, 'I am sick and tired of racial reconciliation.' I know this sounds odd, coming from a pastor who understands forgiveness to be the cornerstone of Christianity, but stay with me. Often, when a black person is racially abused or suffers racial injustice, many white Christians will leap to the reconciliation and forgiveness part and forget their role in making the situation better. The reconciliation that Jesus achieved on the cross was radical, extreme and punishing – it cost Jesus everything. As black theologian Dr Clifton Clark says, 'The social and racial reconciliation we seek – and desperately need – comes at a cost: crucifying the sinful self (Galatians 2.20). Racial reconciliation without such commitment merely provides a temporary sticking plaster to the problem.'[4]

For racial reconciliation to be achieved, for radical solidarity to be realized in the UK Church, black forgiveness of white racial wrongs cannot be the only answer. White confession and repentance also need to happen. Confession and repentance for denying racism exists. Confession and repentance for a lack of impetus to correct racial inequality in the Church. Confession and repentance for ignoring the repercussions of overlooking white privilege. These racial wrongs have to be recognized and addressed. Whether it's the white church member who constantly forgets or mixes up a black person's name on a Sunday or banter that is actually racist, many have gone straight to the forgiveness and reconciliation responsibility of the black aggrieved and failed to acknowledge the obligation of the white offender to repair the relationship. It's this failure from white majority culture that makes forgiving again and again for racial sins so difficult. Black Christians do it because Jesus forgave us for much more, but forgiveness without progress is hard. This is not to say we should not forgive. Rather, my point is that if in doing so we miss the opportunity for inter-racial dialogue, we miss an opportunity for bridges to be built and real change to occur. Failure by the UK Church to make strides to show radical solidarity with those on the margins is one of the reasons that there is a perception, by some people of colour that the UK Church doesn't care about racism.

Biblical radical solidarity

The growth of the black church can be traced back to the prejudice that black people experienced arriving in the UK in the 1950s and 1960s. Migrants from the Commonwealth came to the UK expecting a warm and friendly welcome. What many black people experienced on arrival were churches discouraging them from attending or, in more extreme instances, refusing them admission to their church buildings.[5]

There were exceptions, as we'll explore in Chapter 7, but the overwhelming experience of black migrants seeking to join the UK Church was one of suspicion and rejection, springing from a combination of ignorance, fear and insecurity within it. In 2013, Archbishop Justin Welby made the following comments:

> The Anglicans in the UK did not trust the newcomers, and when they came to church they were not welcomed. The result was that they formed their own churches, as did people from Africa when they came. And the African and Caribbean-led churches today in England are the strongest in the country.[6]

Welby continued by acknowledging that the Church of England was thoroughly unbiblical in its approach to welcoming members of the Commonwealth:

> In those days in the Sixties, we did not recognise that we belonged to one another. That we were called by Christ to love one another. And so the Church of England lost the new life that they brought and that God was trying to offer us through them.[7]

What would the UK Church look like today if, 50–60 years ago, black migrants had been met with a warm welcome and expressions of radical solidarity? What could the Church look like in a generation's time if we commit ourselves to this work now? For better or worse, the leaders set the culture of any organization and the Church is no different. For the Church culture to present radical solidarity in terms of race relations, church leaders have to be at the forefront of change. A great biblical example of this radical solidarity is found in Acts 6. One of the wonderful things about Pentecost – the coming of the Holy Spirit on thousands of people – is that it levelled the playing field. It connected people. Thousands of native Jews and hundreds of Greek-speaking foreign Jews came together in Christ (see Acts 3). All were reconciled to God, no matter where they were from. It didn't immediately remove all the bigotries and biases people held in their hearts, however. This is a stark reminder that even in the context of church, we need to continually work at understanding our prejudices, seeking to build relationships with a diverse range of people.

In Acts 6, the Greek Jews (the foreign minority culture) protested that their widows were not being fairly treated in comparison to those of the Hebrew Jews (the indigenous majority culture) in the distribution of food (v. 1). Greek widows thought that they were being unjustly treated. This was a problem not just because of unfair treatment but because, in Jewish and Christian culture, one of the uppermost principles is the love and care for the most marginalized, defenceless and vulnerable in society (see Isaiah 1.16–17). In this context, it is widows and orphans. This new, diverse Christian family would have held this shared value, but it didn't seem that it was being lived out.

In Acts 6, there is an incredible demonstration of unity and radical solidarity in the way this situation is resolved. The Greek- and Hebrew-speaking Jews come together and the leaders of the early Church appointed seven leaders to supervise the distribution of resources to those in need. What then occurred was intriguing. The Hebrew Jews were the dominant, majority culture, but it was the minority culture that was given authority and responsibility to lead and act in this area of distributing food to the widows. Majority power and control were relinquished. Racial hierarchies were being demolished. This is one of the key solutions to dealing with racial conflict and demonstrating radical solidarity in churches: dismantle existing power structures that cause inequality and injustice. In that one moment, you see trust, love and a deliberate attempt to include those on the margins, levelling the playing field and giving the minority culture a chance to be included and exercise authority.

Minority and majority culture were all in it together to solve the issue and a radical solidarity was achieved. The short-term immediate need was addressed but, also, there was increased meaningful authority given to the marginalized. Power structures based on race and culture were destabilized. At no point was the minority culture first told to forgive and reconcile; the onus fell on the majority culture to actively make the situation right. The minority culture was given responsibility and authority. They were heard, empowered, valued, trusted, loved and respected. As we attempt to live in a diverse society and embrace and accept the beautiful differences in our community, the story in Acts 6 should act as a warning against apathy towards racial disharmony, injustice and bias. The truth is that subtle differences have the potential to foster uncomfortable tension and bring complaints if not exposed and addressed.

Newday

I recently witnessed a powerful expression of radical solidarity. Every year thousands of young people attend the event Newday, camping at the Norwich Showground in Norfolk, UK. The majority of the 7,000 young people are white and middle class. Over the last five to ten years, the demographic has changed, with more black children from inner cities attending. In that period, the Newday leadership team (which I'm now part of) has tried to be intentional and deliberate in making the event more reflective of the changing audience. From worship to seminars, the black Christian experience is now being considered.

During the event in 2016, black teenager Leoandro Osemeke was stabbed to death hundreds of miles away in Peckham, south-east London. The nature of technology and social media meant that the aftermath of the attack and the attempts to save his life were caught on the social media platform Snapchat. Even though Newday was a long way from the incident, within moments, traumatizing news and images of Leoandro's death had spread across the campsite. The morning after the murder, the last Saturday of Newday, would normally have been a time for all 7,000 young people to gather in the Big Top for fun games. Joel Virgo, who leads the event, decided to cancel this tradition and lead the whole site, 7,000 children and their youth leaders, in prayer for Leoandro's family and those young people at Newday impacted by the murder. Joel is white and leads Emmanuel Church in Brighton. The levels of knife crime in Brighton are virtually non-existent in comparison to other major cities in the UK. The vast majority of the 7,000 attendees at Newday that year would not have been directly impacted by Leoandro's murder. While knife crime in the UK can directly or indirectly impact anyone, most of the children in the Big Top – the majority coming from outside of London – would not have been familiar with the level of violence some young people in London are accustomed to. Yet, in that moment, Joel and the Newday team demonstrated radical solidarity with the minority culture. One part of the body of Christ was in pain and the majority culture responded with love and compassion, laying down its agenda to serve the immediate needs of the minority culture. Those suffering felt heard and supported.

This was the beginning of a long-term commitment from Newday to engage with this issue, including financial support for initiatives that can help to reduce youth violence across the UK. While this may seem like an extreme example, responses like this express radical biblical solidarity and are necessary in building an inclusive Church.

Jesus always brought people from the outskirts into the centre and showed them the greatest honour. These ordinary people, through the Spirit of Jesus, ended up changing the culture around them. The socio-economic make-up of Jesus' disciples were people on the periphery of society – tax collectors, fishermen, even extremists. The men and women Jesus connected with most and demonstrated the most compassion for were socially and culturally ostracized. Yet, Jesus brought them into the centre of his world and mission to influence, shape and lead the greatest revolution in history. Steve Addison stated, in his book *Movements that Change the World*:

> In the renewal and expansion of the church, the breakthroughs always occur on the fringe of ecclesiastical power – never at the center. In every generation, in some obscure place, God is beginning something new. That's where we need to be.[8]

For the Church to be all it can and should be, we cannot ignore those on the edge of church life. In the UK Church, this would mean fully embracing people of colour and bringing them into the centre.

The power of love

In May 2018, Prince Harry married Meghan Markle, a mixed race American actress, at St George's Chapel, Windsor Castle. The wedding was a glorious display of diversity – a clash of new and old exploding with all the radiance that a multi-ethnic, hyper-diverse gathering can bring. One of the highlights of the day was undoubtedly the address from Bishop Michael Bruce Curry. Bishop Curry, the first African-American presiding bishop of the American Episcopal Church, delivered a stirring, impassioned message peppered with themes of social justice and civil rights. His message, entitled 'The power of love', captured the hearts of believers and non-Christians. Quoting Dr Martin Luther King Jr, Curry said:

We must discover the power of love, the redemptive power of love. And when we do that, we will make of this old world a new world, for love is the only way . . . There's power in love. Don't underestimate it. Don't even oversentimentalize it. There's power, power in love.[9]

It is this message, the message of Jesus Christ, that the UK Church needs to be reminded of when it comes to race relations. We are to imitate the teachings and actions of Jesus, who showed love to all.

For your consideration

Person of colour Do you find it hard to forgive acts of racism against you? Does the description of the diverse early Church give you encouragement that racial harmony/solidarity is possible?

White church leader Thinking about the example from Acts 6, what steps could you take to demonstrate radical solidarity with the ethnic minority culture in your church?

White church member What would it look like for you to show radical solidarity? What might you do to take steps towards this? What might you need to give up?

Looking in The early Church was known for its radical love and unity. Do you think this is the case today?

6. KICK IN THE DOOR

CHURCH LEADERSHIP

'Diversity is about bodies,
inclusion is about culture.'
DeRay Mckesson
American activist and author

It is often said that if you work hard, you can become anything you want to be. This philosophy is good in theory, but evidence suggests that there are some jobs where working hard still does not grant you access to the top employment positions if you're from an ethnic minority – senior church leadership being one example. It is in itself telling that statistics for the ethnic breakdown of UK Church leadership positions, across the denominations, are hard to come by. The Church of England does collect this data. Recent figures show that 92 per cent of its clergy and 94 per cent of senior clergy are white and British. In 2017, statistics showed that 3.5 per cent of clergy are BAME and, among new ordinands, only 7 per cent were from minority ethnic backgrounds.[2] Clearly there are hurdles to the advancement of black leadership. Black people are seriously under-represented in positions of church authority, influence and leadership. The more responsible the position, the more under-represented we are.

Taking London as an example, nearly half of churchgoers in inner London (48 per cent) are black, 28 per cent in London as a whole, compared with 13 per cent of the capital's population. These statistics show that nearly one in five (19 per cent) black Londoners goes to church each week. Two thirds attend Pentecostal churches and the black community is represented in every denomination.[3] While there may have been an increase in black people across denominations, this does not translate into leadership representation. This leads me to ask whether there are racist structures, including unhelpful stereotypes and unconscious bias, blocking pathways to leadership for black people. The lack of leadership opportunities in the UK is not restricted to the UK Church – the issue is universal. A recent report states:

In the UK today, one in 10 employed people are Black, Asian and Minority Ethnic (BAME), yet only one in 16 of top management positions and one in 13 management positions are held by BAME people. Many UK sectors continue to be closed off to BAME people when it comes to leadership opportunities. Nearly three-quarters (74%) of management positions held by BAME people are clustered in just three sectors: banking & finance; distribution, hotels & restaurants; and public administration, education & health. Yet the majority of management positions within the energy & water, construction, legal, media and political sectors continue to be held by white people.[4]

Representation matters

There is clearly a race problem relating to black representation in senior church leadership positions in the UK. Is there a tendency for only certain 'types' of black people (middle-class, university educated, African rather than Caribbean people, black men married to white women) to be elevated to positions of leadership in churches? Do black people subconsciously concede to white leadership over black leadership, making it impossible for black leaders to lead effectively? Are white congregations naturally resistant to black leaders? Does tokenism trump deliberate and intentional development of black leaders in traditionally white spaces? Is there an expectation for black leaders to adapt, assimilate and conform to white church ideals? Do white-led churches prefer to lead black sheep rather than develop black shepherds? Should white-led churches in ethnically diverse areas implement the words of Earon James when he says, 'Because of the white-centred bent that is inherent in Christianity, if you're going to have something that is genuinely multi-ethnic, I would say it has to be minority led.'[5]

The Bible is a firm advocate of church leadership that reflects the community it serves. One of the best examples of diverse leadership in the Bible is in Acts 13.1, with the leadership team at Antioch. This church leadership team was wonderfully heterogeneous. The team comprised Barnabas from Cyprus and a black man called Simeon (aka Niger, which, as we've seen, is Latin for black). Then there was Lucius, who was possibly black as he was from Cyrene/North Africa. The team also included Manean, who was raised among royalty, and, finally, Paul, a Jew. As R. Kent Hughes says,

> This was the church staff at Antioch – a racially integrated group of go-getters who, Luke says in verse 1, were 'prophets and teachers.' They were a microcosm of what the church would become in the world. This was no accident, but rather a deliberate work of God![6]

The multicultural, multi-ethnic, multinational population of Antioch was reflected in the Church and in the leadership. A mix of different backgrounds, different skills and gifts was a true reflection of the environment. So we know we have a biblical model for diverse and contextual leadership and we see that unity in diversity brings more glory to God. Even so, creating diverse leadership teams remains a challenge for today's Church. When it comes to black people in leadership, there seems to be a struggle and a scrutiny white people do not have to go through. In my experience, black people in leadership or management are seen as a risk (unpredictable, maverick, non-committal), inferior or simply overlooked.

These stereotypical views are prevalent in all walks of life, but are amplified by the mainstream media. The result is that black people in high-profile leadership roles become an anomaly and are therefore open to greater scrutiny. A recent example of media racial bias happened in the world of football. On 2 April 2018, following the dismissal of football manager Alan Pardew from West Bromwich Albion, black former Jamaican International footballer Darren Moore was appointed as the caretaker manager of the Premier League football club. At the time of Moore's appointment, West

Bromwich Albion was bottom of the football Premier league and ten points from safety with six games to complete. Under his leadership, the club went undefeated in April 2018, earning Moore the honour of being awarded Premier League Manager of the Month. Unfortunately, West Bromwich Albion did not get enough points from the remaining games of the season to prevent relegation to the second tier of English football. Moore was the first former Jamaican International to manage in the English Premier League. Moore had proved he could manage at the top level and, on 18 May 2018, he was appointed head coach on a permanent basis at West Bromwich Albion. Moore faced a season in the Championship with the task of returning West Bromwich Albion back to the Premier League.[7]

Large parts of the British media questioned Moore's experience and expertise to do the job full time, even though he had obtained all of the necessary coaching badges and had worked his way through the ranks (working with the under-18 and under-23 football teams at West Bromwich Albion). Two white football pundits for the BBC, Danny Murphy and Mark Lawrenson (both of whom have never managed a professional football club), stated that Moore's appointment would be too much of a 'risk'.[8] Yet, a month on, two recently retired white footballers Steven Gerrard and Frank Lampard both landed high-profile management jobs at Glasgow Rangers and Derby County respectively. Unlike Darren Moore, they had no previous experience of managing professional football clubs. Even so, the reaction from the press was a lot more favourable and encouraging. At the time of writing this, the appointment of Moore at West Bromwich Albion means there are now six black managers out of the 92 English full-time professional football clubs and 30 per cent of football players in the UK are from a BAME background; when you translate that into how many are trusted to manage a club, the figure is only 6.5 per cent. It also means that a generation of black managers has been isolated out of the professional football arena in the UK.[9]

The same pattern of distrust, double standards and racist stereo-typing is apparent in the UK Church. There is a blatant bias towards white leadership.

Stereotyping from the white majority church culture is a problem across the church and is an issue that worship leader Noel Robinson has faced.

I had many stereotypes I had to break through, being a black man, being a praise and worship leader. I'm not here to just sing music but to also train people's lives to acknowledge God. Most people say,'just put a guitar in his hand and strum a few chords and that makes you a worship leader'. Well that's not the case. Christian culture has to wear two lenses. A lens that recognizes what the prevailing culture is and the second lens is what the kingdom culture represents. Oftentimes the prevailing culture is not exposed to minority cultures, therefore stereotypes will build up. For example the word 'gospel' is the preaching of the good news of Jesus Christ. When we talk about Gospel music it is a code word for black musician and the title worship leader could never be given to a black person. My challenge to the prevailing culture was to challenge how they saw and distributed music.[10]

While this issue is multilayered and complicated, part of the problem comes down to an ingrained partiality towards white leadership. The complexity of this issue is something the Revd Les Isaac has witnessed:

There are some races who say 'we're brothers but I'm your big brother'. For the white guys when they meet you they want to know where you were educated, what you studied, what social class you're in before he is seeing your Christendom. In some races and some cultures there is a superiority complex that they have. We have to call that out. We have to realize for some of the tribes and races in this world they believe they have the automatic right to do what they do and they find it difficult for a person of different ethnicity to be over them. That's the reality of the world we live in.[11]

Imposter syndrome and integration fatigue

As one of the few black senior leaders in the movement of churches I'm connected to, two issues that I have consistently fought against, and have seen other black leaders struggle with, are imposter syndrome and integration fatigue. 'Imposter syndrome' is the false belief that you are not as good as everyone else in the room. 'Integration fatigue' is the social and psychological stress responses to being a person of colour in a predominately white environment.

Imposter syndrome is a particular trait that women and minorities often have to contend with. You have finally broken through the locked doors and glass ceilings of the predominantly white male space, you now have a seat at the table and then, suddenly and unexpectedly, all your anxieties come out: 'I'm not as good as everyone else, why and how did I get here? No one else here, either peers or those in authority, looks like me or comes from the same background as me.' You begin to question whether you belong in this once exclusive white (male) space and ask whether you deserve to be in the room. On the one hand, there is the responsibility of people of colour to constantly remind themselves that they bring expertise to the conversation. On the other hand, there is also a duty on the part of the white majority leadership to be as welcoming as possible to the black minority.

I remember, a few years ago, I was invited to join the leadership team of Newday. The leadership, all white, majority middle-class males, had known each other for years. And then there was me. Imposter syndrome hit me. To be fair, the team members did their best to be warm and welcoming and listened to my contributions, but, soon enough, the next issue happened – integration fatigue. As a black leader in a majority white movement of churches, I suffer integration fatigue on a regular basis. This is how it works. I get tired of being the black pioneer in a predominantly white church space. At times I feel exhausted by the struggle of racial integration – trying to build relationships with people who are not like me and do not understand me. I get worn out by being the de facto voice of black people in white settings. I get frustrated at being the only black cultural ambassador in all-white environments. I get jaded by going to church conferences and being literally the only black face. Pastor Steve Tibbert, who was mentioned in Chapter 4 and leads a 1,500 plus black majority church, acknowledges that this is an issue he has seen with some black leaders in his church:

> One of the things I learnt was that if you have one [black] voice, black people feel the pressure to represent the whole of the black community. That person only has one view and is just one person. So that puts a huge pressure on the minority at that moment.[12]

There are further tests and challenges unknown to white people that can challenge the role of the black leader. Edward S. Koh writes:

> Regardless of preparedness, minority leaders and managers face significant barriers within their organisations. These barriers include conscious and unconscious stereotyping, prejudice, and bias related to gender, race and ethnicity, corporate climates that alienate or isolate minorities, lack of mentoring and special or different standards for performance evaluation.[13]

While structural and organizational issues can cause integration fatigue for people of colour, subtle micro-aggressions from white majority culture can make leading in a church environment even more difficult for a black person. I have experienced, as Koh puts it, the 'presumption of incompetence'[14] from white church members, as well as some resistance to leadership. These experiences, combined with personal anxiety, are some of the reasons why integration fatigue becomes a real problem. Black people have legitimate reasons for thinking twice about pursuing a career in church leadership. We become full of self-doubt and often become disheartened and reserved. The complexities behind black people leading churches is, again, something Steve Tibbert has witnessed:

> We have this strange dynamic where the black community has joined King's because it's led by a white pastor. This has been due to a breakdown of trust in the black community in church leadership. Not always, but that has been said to us. What we found over three or four years is that the black community might come in a bit burnt and then they would say to us we really want [black] representation, so that's a challenge.[15]

The complex relationship between diverse congregations and white leadership is something Jahaziel observed while working for the Church of England:

> The funny thing is, one of the churches I worked for was on a north London housing estate with a predominately black congregation, but the leadership was predominantly white. I started to see things, how the [black] elderly people had this automatic deference around the leadership, they would lower themselves around [the leaders] and I was looking at these women who have been flipping soldiers, why are you bowing to him? To see these women acting like that

around the leaders just because he has a dog collar and just because he is white, quite frankly saddened me. But I often see this, particularly with black elders, a built-in, automatic respect for white authority. I would say that it comes from slavery and a post-traumatic impact on how black people view white leadership. It's not just priests and pastors, its doctors, lawyers, teachers, government . . . just an idea that good leadership and whiteness go together – even though our history says otherwise.[16]

The Guinness effect

The lack of senior black leadership in white-led, black majority churches is known in the black community as the 'Guinness effect' – white majority leadership on top, black majority employees or congregation at the bottom.

What I've seen from my anecdotal research is how complicated it can be to develop a racially diverse senior leadership team. There are many factors to this – for example, issues like the practice of unpaid gap-year leadership programmes that can benefit some and be a barrier to those from less wealthy backgrounds. The intern method of employment, which we see frequently in a church context, often leads to a part-time or full-time job. Unpaid internships require a level of financial support from family members rarely seen outside of the white community. One of the ways in which we can address the challenge of all-white leadership is to better understand our natural biases and, in doing so, mitigate their impact. This isn't an easy fix. Our brains are hardwired to make decisions based on past experiences and current perceptions.[17] Raising awareness of this can be helpful, but it needs to happen regularly, including at those points when key decisions are being made. As we see in the book of Galatians, with Peter's recurring bias towards Jewish Christians, we need repeat reminders and the help of God to renew our minds in the area of bias. Often within churches, leadership development opportunities are based on relationship and not on a transparent recruitment policy, which can only make this cycle harder to break.

Modelling

It is my belief that one of the reasons black majority Pentecostal churches are growing rapidly is because people see others like them at the front of the church in the leadership positions and it gives some black people a sense of belonging, commonality, familiarity and trust.

This was definitely my experience joining King's Church London in 2000. Having grown up in a church with all-white leaders, it was refreshing to meet a black leader among the white authorities (at that time, King's was a majority white congregation but did have a black leader on the staff team). That man was Owen Hylton. Owen, who now leads Beacon Church, Brixton, in south London, spent time with me, encouraged me and gave me opportunities white church leaders had never given. My wife and I became Christians at King's in October 2000. By October 2001, Owen had asked us to lead a discussion group on the church's Alpha course. He saw in me something I did not see in myself – leadership – and he gave me every opportunity to run with it, work it out and make mistakes. Consciously or unconsciously, Owen was developing a leadership path for me and other young black men at King's Church. The consequence was that, as Owen continued to develop me, other white leaders began to see me as someone who was on board with the vision and values of the church, and began to give me more responsibilities.

Owen mentored me, prayed with me, challenged me and rebuked me. With Owen, I learned how to pray, how to read the Bible and get to know Jesus. For the first time, I had someone leading me who was not only like me in background and upbringing but also allowed me to see someone who was black and leading in a white context.

I saw a black man preach, I saw a black man go on to lead a church and I witnessed a black man write the excellent book – *Crossing the Divide* – on race relations in the Church. Owen still plays a part in all of my major decisions. As I already mentioned in Chapter 4, we can't become what we can't see. In Owen I saw my future. While this may sound theatrical, I believe it is this level of input that is required for black leadership to flourish in white majority spaces.

I would have given up on church leadership long ago if someone like Owen had not gone through the same battles as me. White people take this level of input and modelling for granted because it's all around them. Noel Robinson comments:

> At a Soul Survivor event, I was invited to teach on music and the prophetic. At the last meeting I did for them, they invited me to lead a song on the main stage. When I came off the stage, the most profound thing happened. In a place where there were maybe 10,000 people, a young black kid came up to me and said, 'I can be a worship leader.' I responded by saying, 'Why are you saying that? Of course you can be.' He said, 'You're the first black worship leader I have ever seen.' That comment is the thing that kept me going. That comment came from a young man's future. This young man and the memory of that conversation 25 years ago is the thing that keeps me going.[18]

Black people have to search for representation of black excellence, black competency, black leadership; the examples are there, we just have to dig deep to discover them because they are not promoted or elevated in mainstream white culture. Having said that, there is a need to challenge the notion that black people can only aspire to roles occupied by other black people. This myth can leave black people feeling boxed in. This reminds me of the scene in Season 2 of the television show *Stranger Things*[19] where Lucas, the black boy in the series, is encouraged to take the role of Winston –

the only black character in the film *Ghostbusters* – for a fancy dress day at school. Lucas remonstrates with his white friend Mike, saying that he specifically did not agree to be Winston. Lucas has the name 'Venkman' (the white scientist) on his boiler suit and so does Mike. After Lucas states all the negatives of being Winston (he joined the team late and isn't particularly funny), things become tense between the two of them. Eventually, Lucas suggests to a stuttering Mike that the reason Mike wouldn't consider being Winston is because he is not black, thus leading to an awkward impasse.

Clearly being *forced* to be Winston – the only black character in *Ghostbusters* – frustrates Lucas, the black boy in the series. It is important to allow emerging black leaders to be themselves while acknowledging that the journey of leadership for black people is not the same as it is for a white person. We do not start at the same starting point and we sometimes require a hand to work through white spaces from those who have navigated the path before us. Without this support, integration fatigue stunts our progress. We need also to acknowledge the importance of hearing from God for direction and the contributions of white allies in the pursuit of racial equality. I can think of two particularly significant moments that have greatly shaped and encouraged me on my path to church leadership; these have both been the words and prayers of white women, one at my baptism in 2001 and one in 2008 on joining Emmanuel Church London. This also serves as a reminder that, when integration fatigue or imposter syndrome occurs, it's important to return to God and remember the calling on your life, which drowns out the voices of doubt.

Assimilation/tokenism

In the predominantly white church spaces I occupy, I've felt that I've had to tread a fine line between assimilation (battling to keep my cultural accent and maintaining my uniqueness) and tokenism (having my individuality instrumentalized for the sake of a white diversity agenda). While assimilation presents a false dichotomy for the person of colour – you're accepted by a white majority culture, but it is not authentic to your own experiences/background – tokenism is nothing but a plaster over the gunshot wound of racism. As a black church leader, soon enough the accusations and criticisms come – from both black and white people. It goes something like this.

- *Black person* That black leader has sold out and is not representing black issues enough.
- *Black person* That black leader only got to the position of leadership because he is African/university educated/married to a white woman/came from a different area from where the church is based.
- *White person* That black leader talks about diversity too much.
- *White person* That black leader talks about issues that impact the black community too much.

As a result, the pressure to be all things to all people can cause burnout. You are perceived as 'too black' for white people and 'too white' for black people. This can leave the black leader in a strange grey, lonely vacuum. Unfortunately, because of the desire of some churches to pursue diversity as a tick box exercise instead of a key biblical principle, some of these accusations are true. Some black leaders will abandon their roots to be accepted – integrating into the majority culture for a perceived more peaceful life. Others will overcompensate just to maintain their standing with the black members of the congregation and the black community. Both of these observations are problematic. I'm aware that by oversimplifying the personalities and characteristics of black people, placing black leaders into two distinct categories is in itself limiting and generalizing. Nevertheless, for me personally, this is a real conflict. The frustration is that we do not naturally define whiteness in such a binary fashion – white people can be what they want, yet black leaders tend to be presented as either Carlton from *The Fresh Prince of Bel-Air* (acceptable to white majority culture) or Malcolm X (the black radical). This leads to what I call black superhero syndrome. Black leaders feel that they have to be the black crusader. The Luke Cage for the black community and the Black Panther for white majority culture. Your dual mission (if you choose to accept it) is to carry the weight of black *and* white expectation because you are a rarity – a black leader in a white space. Now go and save the world.

White church leaders can be the reason for this ill feeling towards black leaders – because of tokenism. 'Tokenism' is incorporating a person or minority group in an effort to appear diverse. The people chosen are usually characteristically and interchangeably used to symbolize an entire collection of people. Within the institution of Church and most well-meaning organizations, you will discover that there's a fine line between having a diverse range of expressions and tokenism.

When putting together a church programme, and considering who should be in church leadership, it's vital that the church intentionally and deliberately discovers diverse leaders from the variety of people represented in the church. We can call this contextualized leadership – this simply means leadership from the culture you're trying to reach, in the culture you're trying to reach. I agree with Pastor Earon James when he says:

In order to create a very Godly and Christlike push back against any type of ethnocentric expression of the faith I think one of the key ways to operate in direct opposition to that is for the majority to learn from, submit to, in terms of elders and teachers, scholarship and preaching, to black people and people of colour.[20]

The lack of racial integration and inclusion in white majority churches suggests that there is systemic racism in the UK Church.

The Bishop of Rochester, James Langstaff, who chairs the committee for Minority Ethnic Anglican Concerns agrees:

> [Some within the Church] hesitate to use the language of institutional racism. We also speak of conscious or unconscious bias, which is slightly less emotive. But it is, in my view, undeniable that there is racism within the system, because gifted people have not found their way into senior leadership[22]

Power

In Chapter 3, I quoted the Revd Duke Kwon on the topic of racial reparation. Kwon said that we needed to repair broken leadership structures that 'try to add diversity without subtracting control'. Kwon calls for us to take more notice of the leadership skills and abilities black church members possess, as often these have been neglected by white leaders. This neglect creates a deficit in black senior leadership in white majority churches. For the UK Church to implement Kwon's words, leadership development for black people cannot be left to chance. A deliberate and robust strategy that gives the minority culture opportunities to lead can only happen when the majority culture is giving away permission to control and shape the culture. This will require white church leaders to relinquish power, champion black people and allow us to develop leadership opportunities for the context, in the context. Only then will the UK Church begin to see the kind of diverse senior church leadership that we see in the early Church.

For your consideration

Person of colour What are your experiences of pathways to leadership in your church? Do you believe that your voice or opinion is heard and well represented? Have you ever suffered from imposter syndrome and integration fatigue?

White church leader In your experience of discipleship and leadership development, are you aware of the biases you carry? What could you do to mitigate their impact?

White church member Do you have experiences of being led or managed by a person of a different ethnicity? Does the person's race play a part in how you respond to the leadership offered?

Looking in Is the ethnicity of the church leader, or seeing people of colour in leadership positions, a determining factor in whether or not you would join a local church?

INTERLUDE

BLACK (WO)MAN IN A WHITE WORLD

'There is a kind of strength that is almost frightening in a black woman. It's as if a steel rod runs right through the head down to the feet.'[1]

Maya Angelou
author and poet

The Revd Dr Kate Coleman has over 30 years of leadership experience as a Baptist minister, is a former president of the Baptist Union, former chair of the Evangelical Alliance and author of *7 Deadly Sins of Women in Leadership*. Kate is also founder and co-director of Next Leadership, an organization committed to developing leaders in the public, private, voluntary and church arenas. I was keen to hear her thoughts and experiences regarding issues of race, gender and leadership in the UK Church.

Have you always felt a calling on your life to be a leader?

I became a Christian at university. After I became a Christian, some of the guys at university asked me to lead a Bible study and that's when I knew I had a thing about theology. I think that's when I developed a thirst for the Bible and leadership.

The real moment of shift came three years later when I finished university and asked the Lord what he wanted to do with my life and I said I would do anything, but I had a few good ideas of my own – unfortunately God wasn't really interested in my ideas. I returned to London from university in Southampton. I had a very clear sense of prompting by the Lord that he wanted me to come up to a high mountain alone with him and he would speak to me there and one day I was reading the Bible where it says, 'Jesus took with him Peter and James, and John his brother, and led them up a high mountain by themselves' (Matthew 17.1). I took that as God speaking to me. So I asked myself, 'Where are the high mountains in the UK?' The next day I was on the London Underground, Chalk Farm station, on the platform. I looked up and there was a poster and a picture of a mountain on it saying, 'VISIT SCOTLAND'. So I said, 'OK, Lord, I'll do that', and went to Scotland for three weeks. I spent the first two weeks praying and fasting, asking the Lord, 'What do you want me to do?' And in that time, God spoke to me really clearly about leadership and the call to leadership in the Church.

What happened next?

There were some challenges. First, the church I was at in Chalk Farm didn't believe in women in leadership. Second, neither did I because that was what I had been trained in. So I had to ask the question, 'Where was this coming from?' I said to the Lord, 'If this is you, you are going to have to make this happen as, (a) I can't believe it's you, (b) this doesn't make any sense to me and (c) our church doesn't believe in women in leadership.' I came back down from the mountain and came back to London. Within three years of my 'mountain' experience, I was leading the church that did not believe in women in leadership.

Can you say a bit more about the process you went through when becoming a church leader?

The first thing that happened when I came down the mountain was that my church leader said, 'Although we do not believe in women in leadership, we would like to offer you a position on the deaconate as a church deacon.' I thought this is what God had meant when he spoke to me about leadership, so I accepted. At that point, the church at Chalk Farm was deciding to go with either the Ichthus or Newfrontiers movement of churches. A while later, we then went into a huge traumatic change in the church because our pastor had to step back due to infidelity. I was suddenly put in the fray to lead the church and was left to deal with the mess. Our overseers instructed me to sort it out, even though these overseers didn't believe in women in leadership at that time.

How did the church respond?

Shortly after this, one of the overseers came down from East Anglia to London and had a meeting with our church and said, 'God has spoken to me about my attitude towards women in leadership and I'm here to repent. I'm repenting in front of all of the churches that I have oversight over and I want to appoint four elders and Kate is going to be one of them.' The church went into meltdown. People didn't mind that I was doing stuff as long as there wasn't any title or official recognition attached to it. During this time, I discovered how badly Christians could behave. There was fallout, backstabbing and the worst behaviour imaginable.

We finally made the decision as a leadership to affiliate with Ichthus rather than Newfrontiers, as they had already developed their theology in a way that included and championed women leaders.

I had to grow up pretty quickly and this was easily the most challenging and difficult season of my life – I was 23 or 24 at the time and had only been a Christian three or four years. Out of that time, I emerged as the natural leader of the church and kept things together as much as I could. Obviously people left, but I guided the church through that period with the other guys who had been deacons but were now elders. They all looked to me and said it is really obvious that Kate's the leader. However, another huge shift and pivotal moment took place in the church a couple of years later. A key white guy in the church called Tony Cummings (a founder of Cross Rhythms and really big in the Christian music industry) stepped up and surprised us all. He wasn't in leadership, but was very well respected. He stood up in one of the church meetings and said, 'I don't know about the rest of you, but as far as I'm concerned, Kate is my pastor.' After that, whenever people brought family or friends to church, they would introduce me to them as their pastor.

So white male validation, a white ally, another white leader or influencer supporting you, was a game changer?

That is often the way it has been for me, but Tony's comments worked on two levels. First, this was a man validating a woman and confirming that he was placing his confidence in me. And, second, here was a white person validating a black person and saying that he recognized authority, grace and gift in me. Before this moment, some of the people were happy to view me in a particular way, but from that moment, everything shifted and changed.

During this same period, people like Les (co-founder of Street Pastors) and Louise Isaac joined Ichthus and turned up looking like African royalty in a sea of whiteness. They were encouraging and very supportive.

It seems that, for you to flourish and survive that period of your life leading a white majority church, you needed a combination of white allies and black encouragement? You needed that balance?

Absolutely, although I would go a step further and say, you should never look for balance. What you need is an immersive space where you don't have to explain yourself. You do not even have to start the conversation, someone else might start the conversation and say, 'Did you see?' 'Did you notice?' You need a place where you can be at home. Even the close white friends I have tend to be 'third culture' people, people who have been raised in another context and understand what it feels like to be a minority in that context, who love and appreciate another culture and who understand what it's like for people who have experienced difficult circumstances and opposition for who and what they are culturally.

Were you thriving?

Yes and no. I was developing and I was learning how to pastor. I hadn't gone through any training at that point. I started training after I had been pastoring two or three years. Nobody in the Baptist Union suggested that I should do any formal training. That encouragement came from elsewhere – places such as the Independent Baptists, the guys at Ichthus and Anglican friends.

Being black in this space was often incredibly hostile. The church was safe and not safe because I still had to be careful about how I pastored some of my white members – men in particular. All the while, I was on an exponential learning curve.

Initially I went to Ichthus to ask to do their training course, but one of the leaders, Simon Thomas, said, 'I've prayed about this and I really feel you need to take the Baptist route.' I was resistant to this because I really did not want to take the Baptist route. The Baptists felt stuffy and old. Anytime I went to a fraternal, I was the only woman there or the only black person there. Most were pretty rude or dismissive and it wasn't a nice space to be in. But, because Simon was saying it and he was a man of God, I felt I better pay attention. I put it to prayer and eventually felt that I needed to do the Baptist training too. Throughout this time, I had space and got involved in loads of other things that interested me. The Baptist emphasis on autonomy probably did a lot to preserve me in those days.

Did you feel supported?

One of my key mentors was Emmanuel Lartey, who was the leading black theologian in the UK at the time. He took me under his wing. I taught on the first black presence in the Bible course in the UK with the Revd Les Isaac, which was called 'Black Light'. All types of people, white and black, came on the course. Then I reconnected with English philosopher, sociologist and theologian Elaine Storkey, who I met at university briefly when she came to speak. She was brilliant on women's issues and gave me a lot of space. Elaine was running the London Institute for Contemporary Christianity at the time and, when I said that I wanted to run a conference called 'Great Africans in the Bible', not only did she put her neck on the line and invite me to use the London Institute of Contemporary Christianity as the venue but she also introduced me to some of her friends from the USA with expertise that also contributed to a successful conference. This was 1989. Elaine has become a great friend and mentor since.

Many of the young leaders of colour I mentor or pastor say that race and gender discrimination are not that bad nowadays. What would you say in response to that comment?

I hear many younger women say similar things, like, 'I haven't had to fight like you to be in leadership positions in church', and I'm really grateful for that, as I (and others like me) had to go through a lot of stuff to make that possible for them. For me, in my time, some of the racism I might have experienced would have had me having dog crap pushed through the door or the police slow crawling us from behind. Things that still happen to some black men today were happening to me back then. Shifting back to gender, when I'm speaking to white or black women, the comment often is, 'the issue of sexism is not such a big issue for us now' and 'we're glad you guys made space for us, but we do not face the same struggles today'. My response is, first, the reason you do not face these issues is largely because, in many of our major cities, we have an urban subculture, which means that white and black mix and share cultures in a way they couldn't back in the day. Second, it's because many of you are still in entry-level leadership so, at that level, there is a lot more acceptance of the shifts and changes that open doors to and for women's leadership. However, as soon as you start reaching more senior levels of leadership, that's when you notice the Guinness effect more if you're black. That's also when you experience the worst glass ceilings and see the fewest women.

The discrimination around gender and race in church leadership is still happening, but it's focused now between middle and senior leadership in most places. When people are based in urban cultures like London, they don't notice structural racism as much. London is very cosmopolitan, but when they work [in places] outside of London, [such as] Birmingham, where people live in parallel or outside the urban hubs of small cities and villages, racism becomes more obvious.

This is when you know it's still a structural reality. I'm grateful that some of the women do not have to do some of the journey that I had to and still have to do, but the reality is, the structural and external stuff is still there. Many of these women will not be noticing the external structural stuff in the same way as in previous years. This is often the same for a lot of black people, particularly in urban contexts where they are interacting with and working alongside white people as equals. But the internalized messages for many young women and men are still the same. They may not notice the structural stuff, but the negative messaging is still being internalized in destructive ways for many. So some of these young women are still struggling with issues of confidence and boundary setting. They are still struggling with issues of a robust life vision, which goes beyond love, marriage and children. They are still struggling with issues of how to manage their time in a world that expects them to be great mothers *and* excellent workers. When it comes to young black people, they are still internalizing negative messages and they still don't see themselves necessarily as equal to white people.

You became president of the Baptist Union and chair of the Evangelical Alliance. What work do you do now?

Some of the work I'm doing now is around leadership development. I also do some diversity training as a lot of the white majority organizations I'm working with have only a few black people and are hearing about the extent of structural racism or sexism for the first time. However, I try not to get pigeonholed in this. My main work is mentoring, coaching and running leadership development programmes, because I have come to appreciate the importance and need for great leadership in and beyond church circles and I am prepared to facilitate the development of pioneering and transformational leaders whatever their sex or race, as long as they are willing to learn from me.[2]

7. JESUS WALKS

SOCIAL ACTION

'You can't understand the important things from a distance. You have to get close.'[1]

Bryan Stevenson
American lawyer, social justice activist and director of the Equal Justice Initiative

'He is dead, Ben. Myron has been stabbed and he is dead!'

Sunday 3 April 2016 is an evening I will never forget. I was away with my family on holiday. That Sunday the call came in around 8 p.m. from Myron's stepdad, a good friend of mine. My wife never likes me answering calls on holiday, so I ignored it. Then the text came through: 'Ben, call me back. It's urgent.' I knew something bad had happened. Then came those 12 words that I will never ever forget: 'He is dead, Ben. Myron has been stabbed and he is dead.' I had known Myron and his family for the best part of 16 years. He was 17 when he was stabbed to death in New Cross, south-east London.

Tragically, due to my time working for local authority youth offending and community safety teams, Myron wasn't the first young person I'd known who had been murdered, but when Myron died, I saw the heartache and pain of his loved ones up close. For the first time I saw the full impact of knife crime, from police investigation to conviction. Throughout the ordeal, one of the big questions I asked was 'where is the UK Church's response to this issue?' Knife crime in London disproportionately impacts black people and is on the rise,[2] yet the response from the UK Church has been slow to non-existent. While some parts of the Church in the USA have historically been voices of challenge to societal injustices impacting black people, the UK Church appears to be silent. The effects of issues such as the increase in racism and hate crime after Brexit, anti-Semitism, Islamophobia, xenophobia, extremism and immigration problems on people of colour are not often seen as pulpit-worthy topics, but they are faced in the daily lives of ethnically diverse communities.

Without engagement with these issues, the aim of a multi-ethnic congregation can often appear shallow or symbolic rather than being of any real substance. Could this apparent lack of engagement from the local church be a clue as to why some black people struggle to feel at home in white majority churches? Can we attempt to build racially diverse churches while ignoring race and systemic racism as factors in societal issues? Can silence on these matters, instead of promoting reconciliation, actually reinforce feelings of alienation and voiceless-ness? Could traditional churches learn and adapt their social action strategies to help create a diverse and integrated congregation? My observation is that ethnic minorities are gravitating to churches that are addressing the needs of their specific communities.

In his book, *Black Muslims in Britain*, Richard S. Reddie explores why a growing number of British black people are converting to Islam. Writing about the impact of black majority churches (BMCs) on social action, he says:

> If one considers the scale of and the depth of the problems affecting the Black community in the areas of healthcare, employment, education, training and skills, housing, the criminal justice system, immigration and asylum, and civic engagement, it becomes apparent that there are not enough BMCs involved in real social action[3]

While Reddie makes a valid point, I would take this further. Why must it be only the responsibility of black majority churches to engage with 'black community' issues? Is it not a mandate for the Church as a whole, black majority or not, to display God's mercy and justice to the most marginalized? Is this not especially true of those churches in inner-city, hyper-diverse areas of the UK? The Bible is very clear on the role Christians are to play in serving the needs of those in less fortunate positions in society. Micah 6.8 says, 'He has told you, O man, what is good; and what does the LORD require of you but to do justice, and to love kindness, and to walk humbly with your God?'

Jesus himself encouraged his followers to 'love your neighbour as yourself' (Mark 12.31). The UK Church has a reputation for doing charitable work very well. Between 1 April 2017 and 31 March 2018, The Trussell Trust's foodbank network distributed 1,332,952 three-day emergency food supplies to people in crisis – a 13 per cent increase on the previous year. Of these, 484,026 went to children.[4] Many of these foodbanks were housed in and run by churches. The Archbishop of Canterbury Justin Welby said, 'National education, many hospitals, most hospices, the majority of full-time youth workers: all these were started with or are run by church and other faith groups.'[5]

While this is phenomenal work, in the light of an increasingly racially diverse society, does the UK Church, specifically white-led, white majority churches, need a more refined approach to social action?

Social justice or social welfare

There is a familiar African proverb about villagers who keep finding floating children in the river at risk of drowning. This strange occurrence happens again and again. The villagers keep on pulling the children out of the river, saving them in the process. Suddenly, the whole community is involved and, while not all the children can be saved, the villagers are congratulated for their efforts. One day, however, someone raises the question, 'But where are all these children coming from? Let's organize a group to head upstream to find out who's throwing all these children into the river in the first place!'

Is the UK Church's approach to social action like the first half of this African proverb? Is there a tendency for the Church to put time, energy and resources in the wrong places – leading to burnout, firefighting and a community dissatisfied with the efforts of the Church because the real societal issues are not being addressed? The first response in the African proverb is social welfare. The longing to save the children in the river is the correct response – nobody wants to see children suffer. The children are drowning and someone needs to help. There is an immediate need and an immediate response is essential. However, the second response is one of social justice. While some people need to provide an immediate response, others need to fight against the structures that are causing the issues – those who are throwing them into the river in the first place. The UK Church has become more accustomed to the first response than it has to the second.

The black theologian Robert Beckford said in an interview that there is a difference between 'social welfare' – serving the needs of the community practically – and 'social justice' – campaigning and advocacy, dismantling and addressing the structures that left the community in dire straits in the first instance. Beckford said:

> So we'll visit men in prison, but we won't tackle the criminal justice system – how race in sentencing works against us – or challenge the media for its persistent criminalising of black youth. I think that is short-changing the community and it's short-changing the Gospel.[6]

Some have argued that the Church and politics should not mix. The Archbishop of Canterbury Justin Welby disagrees:

> You would have thought that we might have learned. Stay quiet, don't collect taxes and keep your head down (and on). The trouble is that's not what Jesus Christ did. He was never party political. No wing of politics – left or right – can claim God as being on its side. But Jesus was highly political. He told the rich that, unlike the poor who were blessed, they would face woes. He criticised the King as a fox. He spoke harsh words to leaders of the nations when they were uncaring of the needy. He did this because God cares for those in need and expects those who claim to act in his name to do the same. That means action – and words.[7]

Welby argues that, in today's uncertain times, with issues such as 'Brexit', the UK Church has incredible opportunities to engage in social action to a much greater extent than we currently do and to present Jesus to those around us.

Speaking truth to power

In the 1950s, the British government invited members of the Commonwealth to help rebuild the UK after the Second World War. As a result, the UK experienced an influx of black people from the Caribbean. But the 'Mother country' was not as welcoming as immigrants thought it would be. Racism was everywhere. It has been well documented that the UK Church was less than welcoming to Caribbeans who came to the UK at that time, but there were exceptions. In 1951, the Church responded to the immigration issue by running a conference specifically looking at the 'issues concerning migrants and migration'. The conference was a cross-denominational event by the British Council of Churches and 'debated the possibilities of integrated social action and welfare issues, in response to migrants arriving in Britain'.[8] The three-day conference brought together charities, government minsters, statutory organizations and professors. The academic Claire Taylor wrote, 'The example of this early conference indicates that churches were leading agencies in their response to migrants. In time, it became clear that even the statutory bodies were often looking to the churches to provide answers and assistance.'[9]

On a micro level, some church members were also meeting new arrivals from the Caribbean off the ships and trains with banners with messages of help and assistance. Church members walked to where the need was. These are examples of the UK Church engaging in both social justice and social welfare. These forward-thinking actions prove that there have been instances of the UK Church acting strategically and operationally to address the needs impacting those facing racial injustice and discrimination. The UK must learn from and build on these examples. It is essential that the Church runs to those in need and not just develop plans with the expectation that people will run to it. The Church needs to be committed also to listening to and learning from the experiences of others, not always offering fixed solutions.

Theology

In my experience, when it comes to social action, particularly issues excessively impacting black people, white-led/majority evangelical churches see it as an additional extra. Unless, that is, it's overseas mission to Africa where 'some well-meaning Christians have a theology of mission that seeks to heal the spiritual and physical suffering of people far away, but pays little attention to needs here at home'.[10] As a black person, I struggle with the continued fascination with and fetishization of black children in Africa, but the lack of interest in black children suffering in the UK. Maybe part of the issue is our theology. Pastor Charlie Dates, in his masterful speech at the MLK 50 Conference, said:

> We are wrong to presume that proper passing of verbs and biblical ideas is in itself enough to hurdle the dark night of racism and injustice. We have perhaps consciously made an assumption that sound doctrine and personal conversion are sufficient to serve the ills of our world.[11]

This comment perfectly summarizes my experience of white-led, white majority, evangelical churches. There is an emphasis on 'personal conversion' over community transformation and renewal. Christian courses such as Alpha focus on your personal relationship with Jesus. With Alpha talk titles such as 'How do I pray?', 'Why and how should I read the Bible?' and 'How can I have faith?', the focus is more on the individual than the collective response to Christianity. Churches miss an opportunity to bring hope into hopeless situations when the focus is solely on personal salvation and not at all on how the Church can serve the local community all around. For example, many black churches I have worked with have developed weekend and holiday programmes that include culturally relevant workshops/projects/retreats for inner-city youth. These workshops help take young people off the streets, divert them from any potential trouble and relieve home pressures. Lunch is provided, which takes pressure off poorer families that can struggle to provide food during holiday periods. Sessions are led by culturally competent staff who understand the inner-city environment and the needs of the young people. Are the different approaches in white and black churches simply down to theology? In a series of tweets, the black American pastor and academic Anthony Bradley claimed that, 'Generally in the black church, you learn about Jesus through Moses. Evangelicals, [through] Paul. That's why Evangelicals struggle with social issues.'[12]

His overarching point is that many black churches promote a theology that leads to Jesus through the Old Testament story of Moses, which tells of a God of justice who hears the cry of his people and saves and redeems them. As a result, black people are presented with the redemption of all things – creation, people and places. However, the majority of white evangelical churches come to Jesus through the Apostle Paul in the New Testament. Here there is a heavy focus on the grace of God for the sinner and the importance of the family of Christ representing the Church. The result is that there is an overemphasis on personal salvation and community renewal is in the shadows. Bradley argues that if your theology and teaching are more Pauline than Mosaic, then it becomes really hard to see how the word of God applies to social justice issues, whereas the Mosaic starting point allows freedom 'to articulate why God cares about personal salvation, economics, business and education, etc'.[13] Historically, that is why people such as Dr Martin Luther King Jr, and black churches in the USA, 'had an easier time making a case for why God cared about slavery, Jim Crow [laws] and civil rights than white churches and therefore did not have to defend Christian witness in society'.[14] Bradley concludes that if you are leading a diverse church, the congregation 'need systematic theologies with the priorities of Moses *and* Paul which culminate in the work/person of Christ'.[15] In other words, 'Christians are called to redeem entire cultures, not just individuals.'[16]

If you lead a church in a diverse area, this should provoke you to consider how to contextualize the gospel. The Church should be presenting the lion as well as the lamb of Jesus' character. People who are struggling to survive day to day need to hear about the God of justice, who will fight on their behalf, as well as the God of grace, who will provide salvation, peace and reconciliation. People need to see action, not just words. I believe the failure of the white-led, white majority churches in diverse communities to communicate the God of justice has contributed to the decline of the traditional Church and the increase in membership of the black Church.

The light

It was in the desperate, hopeless and heartbreaking circumstances of the Grenfell Tower fire tragedy in 2017 that the Church shone a light in a dark situation. The church of St Clements, Notting Dale, offered a refuge for those impacted by the disaster. Grieving families found shelter and were given donations of clothes and food. The community witnessed action over words. The Revd Alan Everett, who leads St Clements, described the moment: 'I was woken up at 3 a.m. by a priest who lives in the tower, and so I came down to the church, opened the doors and turned the lights on.'[17]

This act of love was not lost on the general public or the media. A journalist interviewing the Revd Everett commented on the kindness of the church in this moment: 'Listening to Everett, it struck me that "opening the doors and turning the lights on" was precisely the difference between the church and a local authority'.[18]

I take this profound metaphor of 'opening the doors and turning the lights on' as an encouragement to the UK Church as a whole.

White-led, white majority churches in ethnically diverse communities must fight to engage with issues not just important to white culture. For instance, between 2015 and 2017, seven young people were murdered in the borough of Lewisham – the part of London where my church is situated. All of them were black. As already mentioned, in London, black young people are disproportionately likely to become victims of knife crime. With three of the murders in Lewisham, the church I pastor was able to offer financial support, pastoral care and act as a liaison between the families and local authority. We contributed to funeral costs for two of the families and, in one case, we were able to be a link between the family and our local MP in conversations around the family being rehoused. Our church has continued to support the families long after the funerals and press coverage ceased. In response to these murders, I organized a quarterly prayer meeting called the 'Battle for Lewisham', to create a space for the community to come together to hear from the police, practitioners and people who want to help reduce knife crime. This prayer meeting attracted Christians, people of other faiths, agnostics and atheists from the local community. It was an opportunity to express empathy and encouragement and to listen to and learn from one another.

Through the commonality of our concern about youth violence, we found that we had an opportunity to begin to reduce hostility between local authorities and different sections of the community. Our church has partnered with the youth charity XLP, which has now trained members of our congregation to become local mentors. We also collected financial offerings, which funded local youth organizations to deliver anti-violence workshops in our local secondary school. These experiences have been part of the journey that has led me to form a charity called Power The Fight, which empowers communities to end youth violence through specialist training, workshops and web-based resources. The charity brings a multidisciplinary approach to equip any individual or group working with young people to be part of reducing youth violence in their context.

Another example of a church addressing local needs is the work of Ecclesia Church, which is also based in the borough of Lewisham. In the year 2016 to 2017, the borough had the highest school exclusion rate in London. There were 63 permanent exclusions in the borough's secondary schools – a rate of 0.43 per cent. This is more than double the Londonwide rate, which saw 0.21 per cent of secondary school pupils permanently excluded.[19] Of the residents in the borough of Lewisham, 46 per cent identify as BAME. This rises to just over 76 per cent among schoolchildren.[20] Black Caribbean pupils are around three times more likely than white British pupils to be permanently excluded.[21] These statistics have led Ecclesia Church to act, developing an independent school that helps young people aged 11–16 who are at crisis in their educational experience. Ecclesia aims to engage young people with pathways to learning that have accredited outcomes to facilitate reintegration back into school or progression on to further education or employment with training. Ecclesia works in partnership with the charity Transforming Lives for Good (TLG). This example shows the Church expanding and responding to the needs of the community beyond its current and immediate suffering, delivering social action with a more contextualized approach. Churches like Ecclesia present innovative ways to engage with an issue that impacts black families excessively rather than just engaging with issues pertinent to white culture. Pastor Doug Logan stated in his book *On the Block: Developing a biblical picture for missional engagement*:

Mission does not simply amount to a profession of theological truths in new contexts. We cannot hope for the mere intellectual salvation of community members, abstractly hoping that they will hear our speeches and come to Christ. Instead, we must enter into communities physically and emotionally. We must enter into their suffering and speak the gospel into their individual broken contexts. We cannot effectively serve broken people and bring them the gospel unless we know their brokenness.[22]

Can the UK Church do more than it's currently doing in the area of social reform and justice in a local context? When white Evangelical Church movements decide to plant/launch new churches in inner-city contexts, is there enough focus on serving and understanding the needs of the existing communities? Does church growth, slick worship, generic social action programmes, a cool website and overseas mission/church planting trump making local connections, listening to the needs of local families and developing projects/programmes in partnership with the local community? I believe the Church can be a major force for societal and structural change, but we are going to need to engage with and listen to the people who are suffering injustice.

Jesus was active. Jesus walked. Whether it was to the Temple to challenge the religious leaders or to the sea where working-class manual labourers earned a living, Jesus went and engaged with locals to present his hope, his mercy and his love. Jesus delivered practical help (feeding the 5,000), but also challenged social and political structures that resulted in poverty and suffering (King Herod Antipas and Zacchaeus the tax collector). Jesus walked and then people followed. Jesus engaged with the specific needs of the community, contextualized his message and renewed culture. Is the UK Church willing to do this for racially diverse communities?

For your consideration

Person of colour Can you think of issues that your church fails to engage with that disproportionately impact black people? Are you confident to talk to your leaders about these issues?

White church leader Is your church equipped in understanding the societal issues disproportionately impacting black people locally or nationally?

White church member Do you engage with social action issues that disproportionately impact black people? Do you feel comfortable enough to start a conversation with one or more of your black brothers and sisters in Christ to find out what societal issues matter to them?

Looking in What is your experience of church in the area of social action?

8. LET'S PUSH THINGS FORWARD

WHAT NEXT?

'You don't make progress by standing on
the side lines, whimpering and complaining.
You make progress by implementing ideas.'[1]
Shirley Chisholm
American politician, educator and author

My dream is that, one day, we will live in a post-racial society where people are not defined by the social construct of race. I long for the time when heritage can be celebrated and preserved without defining a person's personal identity, determining his or her place in society or outcome in life. We have already seen that the Bible points to a day when 'every nation, from all tribes and peoples and languages' (Revelation 7.9) will stand before the throne of God as equals. We are far from this future reality.

Afua Hirsh, who wrote *Brit(ish): On race, identity and belonging*, states:

> We cannot achieve this [a post-racial future] until we confront the fact that this is a racial present. We can't just let time and procreation do its work. The fact that by 2050, if the figures are right, more than one-third of the British population will be non-white, doesn't solve anything by itself, it just massively expands the number of people who will be affected by the problem. A problem about which we are in complete denial.[2]

In this final chapter, I want to suggest practical ways in which we can all strive towards racial reconciliation, unity, inclusion and integration in the UK Church. I believe there *are* ways of achieving this without becoming exhausted. Ways of confronting the present reality without losing sight of the hope we have for the future, in the completed work of Jesus Christ.

Black agency

The shortage of empathy and lack of responsiveness from some white Christians is what maintains racial inequality in the UK Church. But this is only part of the problem. We also need to acknowledge that passivity from black people does nothing to dismantle systems of racial discrimination. We need those, and especially those with agency and inroads into white power structures, to take opportunities to challenge racism. White ignorance and black inaction are both forms of racist complicity.

Let me clarify what I mean. I'm aware that there are many black people with wealth, status and influence who do magnificent things for those less fortunate. Many black people in positions of power do great work behind the scenes to fight racial inequality. For example, many black people have become mentors and role models to younger black people. The idea of black agency is not about keeping a scorecard of which successful black person is doing more. Rather, the challenge is to black people who are fearful, detached or passive to begin to speak up in the face of prejudice in the Church. Speaking about her influence, Michelle Obama says, 'If there is one thing I have learnt in life it's the power of using your voice. I have tried as often as I could to speak the truth and shed light on the stories of people who are often brushed aside'.[3]

The same principle can be applied in the Church. If we are to see change, black people who have the ear of white decisionmakers should consider using these opportunities to speak on behalf of minorities who do not have the same access.

In essence, for racial equality to become a reality in the UK Church, some black people will need to put their necks and reputations on the line for the marginalized. Some black believers have settled for a lukewarm version of Christian justice. Not radical but weak, not potent but ineffective. The result: long-term systemic racism in the very place where it shouldn't be – Jesus' Church.

Have some black professionals become too comfortable to care about those feeling the full brunt of racial injustice? Do some well-educated black people prefer not to rock the boat, so as not to be seen as stereotypically rebellious as this might limit their pathways to church leadership? Maybe engaging with racial injustice brings back past trauma? Is there a perceived risk of being seen by white leadership as 'too black' or having a chip on your shoulder by engaging with 'black issues'? Maybe some black people who have good reputations with white decisionmakers are aiming to avoid becoming the 'black superhero' mentioned in Chapter 6? Perhaps they believe that black people who continually suffer racial injustice need to just pull their socks up, lift themselves up by their bootstraps and work hard – just like they did? The issue with this philosophy, as Dr Martin Luther King Jr said, is 'It's all right to tell a man to lift himself by his own bootstraps, but it is cruel jest to say to a bootless man that he ought to lift himself by his own bootstraps.'[4]

Some of the reasons mentioned above are legitimate and well-considered. Talking about race can feel divisive, like opening up painful wounds we all wish weren't there. It's important to recognize that black people will come to a conversation about race looking through a range of different lenses, which may depend on their experiences of racism, nationality or cultural background. That is why it's so important for a range of black voices to be heard. The idea of a single black community is problematic – as already mentioned, we're not a monolith. Black people shouldn't have to be representatives for their race. Black British actor Daniel Kaluuya comments on this, stating, 'I'm not a spokesperson; I'm an individual . . . No one's expected to speak up for all white people. I'm just living my life. I'm a black man, I'm proud of it, but I'm just living my life.'[5]

People like Kaluuya are breaking down barriers through their work. One could argue that this is enough. Black people do not have an automatic interest in race or even an instinctive knowledge of the issues and experiences disproportionately affecting black people. However, in order for us all to thrive in white majority settings, we do need to equip ourselves with the tools to challenge racism. In the same article, Kaluuya goes on to say:

> I don't like race debates . . . It doesn't mean I shy away from it, but I'm not 'interested in race'. It's just something I have to have a deep understanding and knowledge of, because of my

experience, and because I have to navigate the western world. It's something I have to know about first to survive, and then to thrive.[6]

As black people, even if talking about race is uncomfortable and is the last thing we want to do, like Kaluuya, we need to be aware of the issues and be prepared to speak on them when we see injustice. If we are committed to seeing a diverse Church in which everyone is able to flourish, we will need to take responsibility for one another, entering into one another's experiences and using our resources to speak out and tackle inequality when we see it.

We can learn from biblical figures such as Joseph (Genesis 41) and Esther (Esther 4) here. These people had the ear of the ruling class/ majority culture. They worked on behalf of the oppressed and fought against injustice. They were advocates for the poor and marginalized, remembering their heritage. For racial inequality to be eradicated from the Church, the responsibility falls not only on white people to challenge the monolith of racism but also on black people with the economic resources, social status and cultural currency to listen to those with different experiences, step up, speak up and be counted. This will take courage and empathy. Righteous anger on behalf of the oppressed must replace passivity. Failure to engage in this way only strengthens racial structures.

White allies

'But Ben, don't *all* lives matter?'

It was at a church training event that my white friend Livy, in re-sponse to a conversation about the Black Lives Matter movement, asked the above question. It was the summer of 2016 and, in the space of two days, police in the USA had unjustly killed two black men, Alton Sterling and Philando Castile. Police brutality is not a new issue on either side of the Atlantic (see the UK police murders of Dorothy 'Cherry' Groce in 1985 and the 2012 murder of Anthony Grainger as examples). Black Lives Matter is the movement started in the USA that has been the most vocal in speaking out about police brutality against black people. Black men aged 15–34 are between 9 and 16 times more likely to be killed by police than other people in America.[7] Black Lives Matter states on its website, 'We are working for a world where Black lives are no longer systematically targeted for demise.'[8]

My response to Livy was this: obviously all lives matter, but historically, in the USA, it has been black lives that have not been seen to have equal value. The execution of unarmed black people by the police is an extension of the long, brutal and violent history of racism in the USA. I've known Livy for over ten years. Livy and her husband Stu Gibbs (also white) started Emmanuel Church London in 2008. Over the years, Livy and I have had many conversations about race – some awkward, but always leading to a better understanding of race issues from one another's perspectives. What happened next was 48 hours of Livy and I intensely going back and forth via text and email, sending articles, reports, films and blog posts engaging with the issue of police brutality in the USA. This led to Stu and Livy asking me the question: how should we respond as a church? I suggested that it would send a powerful message if we prayed for the USA and the issue of police brutality from the front on a Sunday. I knew that many black people in our church were traumatized by what had been happening in the USA. The obvious person to lead prayer about the issue was me, but I declined and suggested that a white person lead. The reason for this was to make it a whole church issue; a demonstration that when one part of the body suffers, we all collectively share the pain (1 Corinthians 12.26). It's a human issue, not just a black problem. Stuart Baker, who I mentioned in Chapter 2, prayed a heartfelt, rich and empathetic prayer about the racial injustice in the USA. After the service I asked a couple of black people about their thoughts on the prayer. One person commented,

'I was pleasantly surprised and encouraged that the church (which is white majority) would care about an issue like this'. Another person said, 'It was nice that a white person prayed as it demonstrated empathy about minority culture issues.'

The reason why Livy was able to participate in a potentially explosive conversation about race was due to us having over ten years of friendship as a starting point. We know each other; we've spent time together, laughed, cried and prayed together. This was not the first time we have had a discussion about race. People sometimes make the mistake of opening up a very deep, personal and exposing debate without making an effort to get to know the person first. The last thing I need when I first meet someone is to start a conversation about racism! This should be a provocation for white members of the Church to actively get to know black people. This will mean moving from your favourite seat on a Sunday to connect with a black person. You might have to invite someone over for dinner again and again until the atmosphere becomes less awkward. White people may ask, 'Why must I make all the effort?' The answer is easy: you're the majority culture and you are part of the power structure, whether you know it or not.

As the Revd Dr Kate Coleman said, white endorsement for a black person can open doors and change opinion. The idea that white validation is needed for black people to progress may split opinion, but if we are to see racial unity within the Church, black people will need more white allies – white allies who are committed to racial equality and unity. We must not confuse white allies with white saviours (serving black people but with self-serving interests). The fundamental difference between white allies and white saviours is that one listens and has empathy while the other tries to control and dominate. It is important to understand that becoming a white ally is often about what is unseen. For example, there are white parents in our church who are intentional about exposing their white children to literature and toys portraying positive images of black and brown people. Other white friends have invested time and money in causes and charities combating issues that excessively affect black people.

Commenting on the 2017 appointment of Donald Trump as President of the United States in an article for *Sojourners* magazine entitled 'Is this a Bonhoeffer moment?', Lori Brandt Hale and Reegie L. Williams, asked the question, 'In the midst of this current political maelstrom, do you individually or collectively want to be a perpetrator, bystander, or resister? Everything is at stake.'[9]

The German theologian and pastor Dietrich Bonhoeffer, who had a deep care and interest in African American history and the black church, became a member of a conspiracy that was responsible for a coup attempt against Hitler. Twelve years after he became one of the first voices in Germany to offer public opposition to the Nazis, they executed Bonhoeffer as a traitor. Hale and Williams suggest that, as Christians, we all should be challenged by Bonhoeffer's example. So often, when it comes to matters of injustice, we fall somewhere on the spectrum of perpetrator, bystander or resister. Their point is that inaction is a form of collusion. Bonhoeffer decided early on, witnessing the evil ideology of Hitler, to be a resister. The question is this: as a white person, are you brave enough to engage with minority culture issues, stand with your black brothers and sisters and create spaces for them to be heard, included and integrated into the life of the Church? In Bonhoeffer's time it was clear – the Nazi's were the perpetrators and the Catholic Church was the bystander. White people, when it comes to the UK Church, race relations and the issues that impact black people, can be asked the same question: are you a perpetrator, bystander or resister?

My people . . . hold on

If you are black, how do you survive the pressure and strain of operating in predominantly white spaces? The Revd Dr Kate Coleman said, 'What you need is an immersive space where you don't have to explain yourself.' Whether this 'immersive space' is at home with your spouse, at work through a diversity network or with friends, it's important to seek out and invest in relationships with people who get you, understand you and are for you. Not all white people are naive about racism and not all black people are 'woke'[10]. As a black person, sometimes life at church becomes too much, especially if you are the only black person or black representation is minimal. My reactions can vary from rage to sadness to numbness to detachment. So, for survival purposes, I have created sanctuaries. Places of beautiful, rich refuge where I do not have to explain myself to anyone, where I can be unapologetically myself. Where I can explain difficult situations and circumstances and not feel judged. For me this means prioritizing time with my wife and friends who really understand me. These times are refreshing and stimulating. For people of colour to consistently engage in the battle for inclusion and integration in white majority churches, we must create environments where we can heal, recharge, laugh, cry, laugh some more and be honest about our circumstances. These places of sanctuary have saved me from turning my back on white church spaces. Finding a sanctuary can also mean searching for resources – books, music, podcasts, art, films and courses – that discuss and present the black experience, which provide a sense of solidarity, energize you or bring rest.

A friend of mine recently felt God had given him a vision for me. In it, he saw me getting out of my car with a heavy, long trench coat on. As I approached my front door, he saw a coat stand outside. He saw me putting the heavy coat I was wearing on the coat stand. I then went inside and closed the door. The heavy coat and the coat stand were left outside. My friend said he felt the heavy coat was a representation of the issues that I am carrying and engaging in. These included community issues, such as youth violence and racial injustice. His point was that, although the burdens and issues the coat represented were things I enjoyed finding solutions for, there are times when I need to put these things down and rest. I need to be mindful that the battle against social injustice does not dominate and consume my whole life.

The temptation can be for issues of racial inequality to be front and centre of all we do. We tweet about it, we blog about it, we watch films and read books about it. We flood and feed our minds, trying to tackle this issue, to the point that every white person is a potential threat and every discussion we have involves deconstructing racial structures. We can become exhausted and drained. As Christians, we need to be aware that while racism should be attacked, called out and tackled, it can never be the focus of our existence and become all-consuming. Protesting racism should not become an idol or a false god. Speaking decades after contributing to the civil rights movement in the USA, the singer Nina Simone, who had suffered from crippling depression, was asked the question regarding how far the civil rights movement had come. Her response:

> 'There aren't any civil rights,' Simone says.
> 'What do you mean?' the bemused interviewer asks.
> 'There is no reason to sing those songs, nothing is happening,' Simone replied.
> 'There's no civil-rights movement. Everybody's gone.'[11]

There was clearly a sense of regret and disappointment that she had put so much energy into something that, in her view, had cost her fame, fortune, friends and, most importantly, her mental well-being. I've known black people to leave churches, lose friends, become bitter and neglect their families because of a lack of boundaries in the area of tackling racism in the Church. If we do not believe the wisdom of 1 Peter 5.7 – that we need to cast our cares on him – the burden of racial injustice becomes too much to bear. The evil of racism robs us of hope; it will govern our thinking and rule our lives. There are certainly moments when we should put the heavy coat on and fight the power of racism in the strength of Jesus our conquering lion. Then there are times when we are to leave the coat outside, close the door and rest in green pastures with Jesus, our Shepherd. We are to look after ourselves and not neglect the wellness of our mind, body and soul in our fight against racial injustice. We need to exercise, eat well and disengage from social media once in a while. It can also be helpful to seek culturally competent therapy – therapists or counsellors with experience of working with culturally diverse clients (even if there is nothing wrong). Above all, seek the word of God, pray and remember to leave the heavy coat outside the front door. It will always be there tomorrow.

Fight the power or power the fight?

In 1989, the black filmmaker Spike Lee made the now legendary film *Do the Right Thing*. Set in summertime Brooklyn, USA, the film chronicles the racial tensions within the hyper-diverse communities and the relationship with the New York police department. The climax of the film is tragic, blistering and ferocious. The lead song of the soundtrack, 'Fight the power' is by the group Public Enemy. With lyrics such as that freedom of speech is 'freedom or death' and we need to 'fight the powers that be', the song perfectly depicts the struggle against racial discrimination that, unfortunately, has continued in the USA and here in the UK. I was recently praying and sensed that, while we are called to fight the powers of injustice, racism, sexism and many other forms of discrimination, to be sustainable and effective, we need to consider how we power that fight. As Christians, we are told in the book of Ephesians that, 'we do not wrestle against flesh and blood, but against the rulers, against the authorities, against the cosmic powers over this present darkness, against the spiritual forces of evil in the heavenly places.' (Ephesians 6.12).

Racism falls into the category of 'present darkness' and, therefore, if racism is evil and there is a spiritual dynamic to its outworking, racial injustice must be tackled first and foremost with the spiritual weapons God gives us – one being prayer. As it says in Ephesians 6.18, we should be 'Praying at all times in the Spirit, with all prayer and supplication. To that end keep alert with all perseverance, making supplication for all the saints.'

Prayer opens and reveals the issues of the human heart. Prayer can lead to repentance and forgiveness. Often when we are open to God speaking to us, he will direct us in unexpected ways. Acts 10 gives an example of the power of prayer in crossing cultural and racial divides. The story describes an interaction between three characters: God, Peter (a Jewish man, a disciple of Jesus and a leader in starting the early Church) and Cornelius (a Roman military captain, a Gentile). The story begins with Cornelius praying and hearing God pointing him towards the home of Peter. At the same time, Peter is praying and receives a revelation from God relating to the Jewish commandments concerning food. This vision challenges Peter's prejudice towards Gentiles (non-Jews). The revelation leads God to say to Peter in verse 15 'What God has made clean, do not call common.' It is a fascinating interaction in which two strangers head towards an encounter with one another; people who would normally detest each other because of their racial backgrounds and histories. Yet, because of God's intervention, and their obedience to God's promptings, we observe an encounter that becomes a catalyst for a striking display of solidarity, reconciliation and unity. This meeting results in Peter saying to Cornelius, 'Truly I understand that God shows no partiality, but in every nation anyone who fears him and does what is right is acceptable to him.' (vv. 34–5).

Peter the Jew shares the good news of Jesus with Cornelius the Gentile and his family. This is meaningful for many reasons, but mainly because Peter's heart was exposed to his hidden prejudice towards the Gentiles. This encounter became the impetus and trigger for the message of Jesus to be shared outside the Jewish community. From this story, three things are clear. First, Peter's prejudice was an obstruction to the message of Jesus spreading beyond the majority culture. Second, the story shows a correlation between our attitudes towards inclusion and the potential for monoculture in Christianity. Third, the apathy towards diversity or laziness in crossing racial divides are limiting factors in terms of people becoming Christians.

In our quest to have a Church that truly represents the heart of Jesus, real and hard questions need to be asked. As a white Christian, what shapes your views or expectations of people of colour? Like Peter, is it possible that your attitudes towards people of colour are the blockage to racial diversity and radical solidarity developing in your church? Until Peter had the interaction with Cornelius, Christianity had only connected with the Jewish population. For ten years, the Church was slow in reaching out to the Gentiles. God's revelation to Peter of his desire for inclusivity resulted in exponential growth for the next 2,000 years. However, more than just a numerical gain, the impetus to cross the divide for reconciliation and acceptance was modelled first and foremost by Jesus (see Philippians 2, Romans 5.10, Colossians 1.20–22).

As Christians, we are to model the sacrificial, inclusive, impartial, humble approach of Jesus and be intentional in crossing the racial divides in our communities. For this to happen, we are going to need the help of the Holy Spirit, who produces 'love, joy, peace, patience, kindness, goodness, faithfulness, gentleness, self-control' (Galatians 5.22–23). There is no point in having a loving attitude towards God if we have a hateful or indifferent stance towards people made in his own image. The health of the UK Church depends on all our hearts becoming more like the heart of Jesus.

We must power the fight against racism with prayer. If we power the fight against racial injustice with willpower, hard work, protest and activism alone, we will become exhausted. Prayer gives the battle over to Jesus. Prayer fuels our action. Through prayer, Jesus will give us strength, truth, wisdom, peace, insight, love, forgiveness and power. Through prayer, God wins the main battleground – the human heart. As Christians, we are called to fight the power of inequality and injustice. We are also called to power that fight with prayer. Let's combine prayer and action to rid the UK Church and our own hearts of prejudice and racism.

Unmuted

As mentioned in the Introduction, talking about race is hard. In my experience, when approaching the topic of race, many black people feel there is a need to broaden and deepen the usual conversations, bringing in historic issues (such as slavery), cultural observations (such as white privilege) and structural blockages (such as institutional racism). White people tend to steer the conversation to the specific ('I can't be blamed for the sins of my ancestors'), personal ('I've never said anything racist') or procedural ('there's no such thing as structural racism'). Just because a white person doesn't see racism in his or her everyday life, doesn't mean that it doesn't exist. We cannot talk about the present without discussing the past. As frustrating as it might be for a white person to hear about historic events that occurred long before they were born, for black people, it's an important part of the dialogue in moving forwards. White people need to become better listeners to their black brothers and sisters – that is, listening without always offering solutions or making swift assumptions. Black people need to be empowered to move away from being passive bystanders and towards becoming agents of change. If you are black, let me say to you: you're not imagining the issues, you have not got a chip on your shoulder, you have the right to call things out and, when you do, you're not being aggressive. Unmute your voice and prayerfully speak against racial injustice in your church context.

With the rise of the far right globally and the spike in hate crime nationally following the vote to leave the European Union, now is the time for the Church to shine a light on the darkness of racism. Jesus is the light. Our job is to allow his light to reveal any darkness in our own hearts and reflect the light of Jesus to others. We must not let fear prevent us from considering the difficult issues of racism in the Church and beyond. The stakes are too high. The world around us is in desperate need of displays of racial unity and a multicoloured picture of hope. I believe the Church of Jesus Christ has the power to be this witness. How do we get there? It will be a long and difficult journey, but we can start by talking about race.

For your consideration

Person of colour Do you have an 'immersive space' where you can recharge and be energized while dealing with everyday racism?

White church leader What do you see as the qualities of a good ally? How could you and your congregation embody these qualities in solidarity with your black brothers and sisters?

White church member Do you see yourself as a white ally in challenging the structures of racism in your church and beyond?

Looking in How do you think some of the ideas I've presented in this chapter (black agency, white allies, finding an immersive space) could relate to you in your context?

BIBLIOGRAPHY

Akala (2018) *Natives: Race and class in the ruins of Empire* (London: Two Roads).

Alexander, Michelle (2012) *The New Jim Crow: Incarceration in the age of colourblindness* (New York: The New Press).

Anderson, Dr David A. (2010) *Gracism: The art of inclusion* (Downers Grove, Illinois: IVP).

Andrews, Kehinde (2018) *Back to Black: Retelling black radicalism for the 21st century* (London: Zed Books).

Baldwin, James (1963) *The Fire Next Time* (London: Penguin).

Barron, Jessica M. and Williams, Rhys H. (2017) *The Urban Church Imagined: Religion, race, and authenticity in the city* (New York: New York University Press).

Bradley, Anthony B. (2010) *Liberating Black Theology: The Bible and the black experience in America* (Wheaton, Illinois: Crossway).

Burton, Keith Augustus (2007) *The Blessings of Africa: The Bible and African Christianity* (Downers Grove, Illinois: IVP Academic).

Burton, Michael C. (2008) *Deep Roots: The African/black contribution to Christianity* (New York: iUniverse).

Channing Brown, Austin (2018) *I'm Still Here: Black dignity in a world made for whiteness* (New York: Convergent Books).

Coates, Ta-nehisi (2015) *Between the World and Me* (Melbourne: Text Publishing).

Coates, Ta-nehisi (2017) *We Were Eight Years in Power: An American tragedy* (London: Penguin).

Coleman, Kate (2010) *7 Deadly Sins of Women in Leadership: Overcome self-defeating behaviour in work and ministry: Volume 1* (Birmingham: Next Leadership Publishing).

Cone, James H. (2011) *The Cross and the Lynching Tree* (New York: Orbis).

Crouch, Andy (2016) *Strong and Weak: Embracing a life of love, risk and true flourishing* (Downers Grove, Illinois: IVP).

Eddo-Lodge, Reni (2017) *Why I'm No Longer Talking to White People about Race* (London: Bloomsbury).

Ellis Jr, Carl F. (1996) *Free at Last: The gospel in the African-American experience* (Downers Grove, Illinois: IVP).

Emerson, Michael O. and Smith, Christian (2000) *Divided by Faith: Evangelical religion and the problem of race in America* (Oxford: Oxford University Press).

Fanon, Frantz (1967) *Black Skin, White Mask* (London: Grove Press).

Fryer, Peter (1984) *Staying Power: The history of black people in Britain* (London: Pluto).

Hirsch, Afua (2018) *Brit(ish): On race, identity and belonging* (London: Jonathan Cape).

Hylton, Owen (2009) *Crossing the Divide: A call to embrace diversity* (Nottingham: IVP).

Jagessar, Michael N. and Reddie, Anthony G. (eds) (2014) *Black Theology in Britain: A reader* (Abingdon: Routledge).

Keller, Timothy (1997) *Ministries of Mercy: The call of the Jericho Road* (New Jersey: P&R Publishing).

Keller, Timothy (2010) *Generous Justice: How God makes us just* (London: Hodder & Stoughton).

Koh, Edward S. (2013) 'Overcoming cultural and systemic challenges: Exploring how minority pastors overcome leadership challenges in majority culture congregations'. Dissertation for doctorate, Covenant Theological Seminary, St Louis, Missouri.

Logan, Doug (2016) *On the Block: Developing a biblical picture for missional engagement* (Chicago, Illinois: Moody Publishers).

Loritts, Bryan (2014) *Letters to a Birmingham Jail: A response to the words and dreams of Dr. Martin Luther King, Jr.* (Chicago, Illinois: Moody Publishers).

McKesson, Deray (2018) *On the Other Side of Freedom: The case for hope* (New York City: Viking).

Meredith, Martin (2014) *The Fortunes of Africa: A 5,000-year history of wealth, greed and endeavour* (London: Simon & Schuster).

Olusoga, David (2016) *Black and British: A forgotten history* (London: Macmillian).

Perkins, John M. (2018) *One Blood: Parting words to the Church on race* (Chicago, Illinois: Moody Publishers).

Reddie, Richard S. (2009) *Black Muslims in Britain: Why are a growing number of young black people converting to Islam?* (Oxford: Lion Hudson).

Shukla, Nikesh (2016) *The Good Immigrant* (London: Unbound).

Stevenson, Bryan (2015) *Just Mercy: A story of justice and redemption* (Victoria, Australia: Scribe).

Sweeney, Charlotte and Bothwick, Fleur (2016) *Inclusive Leadership: The definitive guide to developing and executing an impactful diversity and inclusion strategy* (Harlow: Pearson).

Wallis, Jim (2016) *America's Original Sin: Racism, white privilege, and the bridge to a new America* (Grand Rapids, Michigan: Brazos Press).

Younge, Gary (2010) *Who are we? And should it matter in the 21st century?* (London: Viking).

X, Malcolm and Haley, Alex (1965) *The Autobiography of Malcolm X* (London: Penguin).

SONG CREDITS

Each of the chapter titles has been inspired by a song.

Introduction: 'I carried this for years' by Ibeyi
Chapter 1: 'Is it because I'm black?' by Syl Johnson
Chapter 2: 'Family feud' by JAY-Z featuring Beyoncé
Chapter 3: 'Why black man dey suffer' by Fela Kuti
Chapter 4: 'You don't see us' by the Roots
Interlude: 'Don't touch my hair' by Solange
Chapter 5: 'Love like this' by Faith Evans
Chapter 6: 'Kick in the door' by the Notorious B.I.G
Interlude: 'Black man in a white world' by Michael Kiwanuka
Chapter 7: 'Jesus walks' by Kanye West
Chapter 8: 'Let's push things forward' by the Streets

NOTES

Introduction

1 <https://denofcinema.com/accept-obvious-r-p-dick-gregory/>, accessed September 2018.

2 Brierley Consultancy (2017) *UK Church Statistics Number 3, 2018 Edition.*

3 Dr Martin Luther King Jr (17 April 1960) *Meet the Press.*

4 Reni Eddo-Lodge (2017) *Why I'm No Longer Talking to White People about Race*, p. 86.

5 Robert McAfee Brown (1988) *Spirituality and Liberation: Overcoming the great fallacy*, p. 136.

6 James H. Cone (2011) *The Cross and the Lynching Tree*, p. 47.

1 Is it because I'm black?

1 Damien Gayle (2018) 'UK has seen "Brexit-related" growth in racism, says UN representative', *The Guardian*, 11 May (available online at: <www.theguardian.com/politics/2018/may/11/uk-has-seen-brexit-related-growth-in-racism-says-un-representative>, accessed May 2018.

2 Stephen Lawrence (13 September 1974–22 April 1993) was a black British teenager from Plumstead, south-east London, who was murdered in a racially motivated attack while waiting for a bus in Well Hall, Eltham on the evening of 22 April 1993 (see: <www.bbc.co.uk/news/uk-26465916>, accessed March 2019).

3 Ta–Nehisi Coates (2017) *We were Eight Years in Power: An American tragedy*, p. 196.

4 BBC (2018) 'Reflecting the ethnic diversity of the UK within the BBC workforce' (available online at: <www.bbc.co.uk/diversity/strategy/bame-career-progression-and-culture-report>, accessed November 2018).

5 J John (2018) 'J John: 5 reasons Christians should fight political correctness', *Premier Christianity*, 9 July 2018 (available online at: <www.premierchristianity.com/Blog/J.

John-5-reasons-Christians-should-fight-political-correctness>, accessed July 2018).

6 Reni Eddo-Lodge, *Why I'm No Longer Talking to White People about Race*, p. 192.

7 Cabinet Office (2017) 'Race disparity audit: Summary findings from the ethnicity facts and figures website, October 2017 (revised March 2018), p. 8 (available online at: <www.ethnicity-facts-figures.service.gov.uk/static/race-disparity-audit-summary-findings.pdf>, accessed March 2018).

8 Persistent poverty is having less than 60 per cent of median income (before housing costs).

9 Cabinet Office (2017) 'Race disparity audit: Summary findings from the ethnicity facts and figures website, October 2017 (revised March 2018), p. 9 (available online at: <www.ethnicity-facts-figures.service.gov.uk/static/race-disparity-audit-summary-findings.pdf>, accessed March 2018).

10 Kehinde Andrews (2018) 'Why do black male graduates earn £7,000 less per year than their white peers?', *The Guardian*, 18 July 2018 (available online at:< https://amp.theguardian.com/world/shortcuts/2018/jul/18/why-do-black-male-graduates-earn-7000-less-per-year-than-their-white-peers?__twitter_impression=true>, accessed July 2018).

11 Simon Burgess and Ellen Greaves, University of Bristol, CMPO (2009) 'Test scores, subjective assessment and stereotyping of ethnic minorities',September 2009, p. 2 (available online at: <www.bristol.ac.uk/media-library/sites/cmpo/migrated/documents/wp221.pdf>, accessed April 2018).

12 Simon Burgess and Ellen Greaves, 'Test scores, subjective assessment and stereotyping of ethnic minorities', p. 23.

13 Lizzie Dearden (2016) 'The Sun and Daily Mail accused of "fuelling prejudice" in report on rising racist violence and hate speech in UK', *Independent*, 8 October 2016 (available online at: <www.independent.co.uk/news/media/press/

the-sun-and-daily-mail-fuelling-prejudice-racist-violence-hate-crime-speech-uk-ecri-report-a7351856.html>, accessed June 2018).

14 Speech by the then prime minister the right honourable Tony Blair MP at Cardiff city hall, the Callaghan memorial lecture, Wednesday 11 April 2007 (available online at: <http://image.guardian.co.uk/sys-files/Politics/documents/2007/04/11/blairlecture.pdf>, accessed May 2018).

15 Gary Younge (2018) 'The radical lessons of a year reporting on knife crime', *The Guardian*, 21 June 2018 (available online at: <www.theguardian.com/membership/2018/jun/21/radical-lessons-knife-crime-beyond-the-blade>, accessed June 2018).

16 <www.ajc.com/news/national/what-happened-charlottesville-looking-back-the-anniversary-the-deadly-rally/fPpnLrbAtbxSwNI9BEy93K/>, accessed September 2018.

17 Trump responds to Charlottesville violence with vague statements blaming 'many sides' (available online at: www.latimes.com/politics/la-pol-updates-trump-tweets-charlottesville-violence-htmlstory.html>, accessed March 2019).

18 The National Child Traumatic Stress Network (2011) 'Secondary traumatic stress: A fact sheet for child-serving professionals (available online at: <www.nctsn.org/sites/default/files/resources/fact-sheet/secondary_traumatic_stress_child_serving_professionals.pdf>, accessed March 2019).

19 Reni Eddo-Lodge, *Why I'm No Longer Talking to White People about Race*, pp. 223–4.

20 See the transatlantic slave trade, apartheid, Jim Crow laws, 'The McPherson report', hostile immigration laws, disproportionate incarceration rates in the UK and US and the UK 'Race disparity audit' for evidence.

21 Reni Eddo-Lodge, *Why I'm No Longer Talking to White People about Race*, p. 87.

22 Safehouse Progressive Alliance for Non Violence (2005) 'Building multi-ethnic, inclusive and anti-racist organization: Tools for

the liberation packet for anti racist activists, allies and cultural thinkers', p. 5 (available online at: <issuu.com/wholecommunities/docs/120801214750-b18b419332c447f88d63d00062588b92>, accessed February 2018).

23 Bill Hybels (2006) *Just Walk Across the Room: Simple steps pointing people to faith* (Grand Rapids, Michigan: Zondervan).

2 Family feud

1 Charlie Brinkhurst Cuff, 'What white people say about us behind our backs, *Consented* magazine, Issue 4, Race and empire, p. 15.

2 'The ANC is a typical terrorist organisation . . . Anyone who thinks it is going to run the government in South Africa is living in cloud-cuckoo land', Margaret Thatcher, speaking in 1987, quoted in Anthony Bevins (1996) 'Nelson Mandela: From "terrorist" to tea with the Queen', *Independent,* 8 July 1996 (available online at: www.independent.co.uk/news/world/from-terrorist-to-tea-with-the-queen-1327902.html, accessed April 2018).

3 Isaac Adams (2015) 'Why white churches are hard for black people', 25 September 2015 (available online at: <www.9marks.org/article/why-white-churches-are-hard-for-black-people/>, accessed January 2018). Cole Brown 'Jesus is not colorblind' (available online at: <www.thegospelcoalition.org/article/jesus-isnt-colorblind/>, accessed March 2019). Darryl Williamson, *I'm not racist; I'm color blind* (available online at: <https://vimeo.com/222004500>, accessed March 2019).

4 Isaac Adams (2015) 'Why white churches are hard for black people'.

5 Aubrey Sequeira (2015) 'Re-Thinking homogeneity: The biblical case for multi-ethnic churches', 25 September 2015 (available online at: <www.9marks.org/article/re-thinking-homogeneity-the-biblical-case-for-multi-ethnic-churches>, accessed August 2018).

6 Aubrey Sequeira (2015) 'Re-Thinking homogeneity: The biblical case for multi-ethnic churches'.

7   James Norriss (2011) 'Othering 101: What is othering', on website;
    There are no others, a catalogue of 'Othering', 28 December
    2011 (available online at: <https://therearenoothers.wordpress.
    com/2011/12/28/othering-101-what-is-othering/>, accessed
    February 2018).

8   Ta-Nehisi Coates (2017) *We Were Eight Years in Power: An
    American tragedy*, p. 54.

9   The title of Frantz Fannon's classic book on race, *Black Skin, White
    Masks*.

10 Ghetts (2018) 'Pick up the phone', from his album *Ghetto Gospel:
    The New Testament* (GIIG).

11 Ta-Nehisi Coates *We Were Eight Years in Power: An American
    tragedy*, p. 54.

12 Carl F. Ellis Jr (1996) *Free at Last: The gospel in the African-
    American experience*, pp. 151–2.

13 Kesiena Boom (2018) '100 ways white people can make life less
    frustrating for people of colour', *Broadly*, 19 April 2018 (available
    online at: <https://broadly.vice.com/en_us/article/ne95dm/how-
    to-be-a-white-ally-to-people-of-color>, accessed March 2018).

14 Reni Eddo-Lodge (2017) *Why I'm No Longer Talking to White
    People about Race*.

15 Reni Eddo-Lodge (2017) *Why I'm No Longer Talking to White
    People about Race*.

16 Stuart Baker (1 February 2018), interviewed by Ben Lindsay.

17 JAY-Z featuring Beyoncé (2018), 'Family feud' from his album *4:44*
    (Rocnation).

3 Why black man dey suffer

1   James H. Cone (2011) *The Cross and the Lynching Tree*, p. 106.

2   Malcolm X with Alex Haley (1965) *The Autobiography of Malcolm
    X*, p. 139.

3   Richard Reddie (2007) 'Atlantic slave trade and abolition', BBC
    News, 29 January 2007 (available online at: <www.bbc.co.uk/

religion/religions/christianity/history/slavery_1.shtml>, accessed April 2018).

4 Richard Reddie 'Atlantic slave trade and abolition'.

5 Martin Meredith (2014) *The Fortunes of Africa: A 5,000 year history of wealth, greed and endeavour*, pp. 78–9.

6 Anthony B. Bradley (2010) *Liberating Black Theology: The Bible and the black experience in America*, p. 127.

7 Anthony B. Bradley, (2010) *Liberating Black Theology*, p. 127.

8 Katharine Reid Gerbner (2013) 'Christian slavery: Protestant missions and slave conversion in the Atlantic world, 1660–1760', doctoral dissertation, Harvard University, p. 5 (available online at: <https://dash.harvard.edu/bitstream/handle/1/11095959/Gerbner_gsas.harvard_0084L_10949.pdf?sequence=3&isAllowed=y>, accessed April 2018).

9 Kris Manjapra (2018) 'When will Britain face up to its crimes against humanity?', *The Guardian*, 29 March 2018 (available online at: <www.theguardian.com/news/2018/mar/29/slavery-abolition-compensation-when-will-britain-face-up-to-its-crimes-against-humanity>, accessed April 2018).

10 Kris Manjapra 'When will Britain face up to its crimes against humanity?'.

11 Leah Cowan (2017) 'Bound together: Personal reflections on Britain's colonial relationship with Jamaica', *Consented* magazine, Winter.

12 Jahaziel (8 March 2018) interviewed by Ben Lindsay.

13 Caroline Davies (2015) 'How do we know David Cameron has slave owners in family background?', *The Guardian*, 29 September 2015 (available online at: <www.theguardian.com/world/2015/sep/29/how-do-we-know-david-cameron-has-slave-owning-ancestor>, accessed March 2019).

14 Martin Meredith, *The Fortunes of Africa*, p. xiv.

15 Martin Meredith, *The Fortunes of Africa*, p. xv.

16 Martin Meredith, *The Fortunes of Africa*, p. xvii.

17 David Olusoga (2018) 'The Treasury's tweet shows slavery is still misunderstood', *The Guardian*, 12 Feburary (available online at: <www.theguardian.com/commentisfree/2018/feb/12/treasury-tweet-slavery-compensate-slave-owners>, accessed March 2019).

18 Erykah Badu (2017) on 'Yellow Fever', Linear notes from *Fela Kutide 4 Vinyl Box Set* (Knitting Factory Records).

19 Two.AM (2017) 'Physicality and crafting the black male identity', 22 December (available online at: <www.two-am.org/opinion-1/2017/12/22/physicality-and-crafting-the-black-male-identity>, accessed May 2018).

20 Ahmed Olayinka Sule (2015) '#LoveSerenaHateRacism: A discourse on Western attitudes towards Serena Williams', Media Diversified, June 8 (available online at: <https://mediadiversified.org/2015/06/08/loveserenahateracism-a-discourse-on-western-attitudes-towards-serena-williams/>, accessed May 2018).

21 John Entine (2000) *Taboo: Why black athletes dominate sports and why we are afraid to talk about it*, Chapter 1 (available online at: <https://archive.nytimes.com/www.nytimes.com/books/first/e/entine-taboo.html>, accessed May 2018).

22 <www.bbc.co.uk/news/magazine-35240987>, accessed March 2019.

23 John Entine, *Taboo*.

24 David Smith (2006) 'Blair: Britain's "sorrow" for shame of slave trade', 26 November, *The Guardian*.

25 Stephen Bates (2006) 'Church apologises for benefiting from slave trade', 9 February, *The Guardian*, (available online at: <www.theguardian.com/uk/2006/feb/09/religion.world>, accessed March 2019).

26 Q Ideas (2018) *Q&A: Race reparations with Pastor Duke Kwon*, 14 June (available online at: <https://vimeo.com/275016018>, accessed June 2018).

27 Q Ideas *Q&A*.

28 Q Ideas *Q&A*.

29 Q Ideas *Q&A*.

30 Q Ideas *Q&A*.

31 Q Ideas *Q&A*.

32 Q Ideas *Q&A*.

4 You don't see us

1 <www.elegantbrain.com/edu4/classes/readings/100readings/ Garvey_bio.pdf>, accessed March 2019.

2 The Secret Teacher (2018) 'Secret teacher: The UK has a complex racial history. Why aren't we teaching it?', 20 January, *The Guardian* (available online at: <www.theguardian.com/teacher-network/2018/jan/20/secret-teacher-uk-history-of-race-bloody-racism>, accessed September 2018).

3 Matthew Philips (2016) 'Art: Whitewashing Jesus', 8 December, *Newsweek*, US Edition (available online at: <www.newsweek.com/ art-whitewashing-jesus-105409>, accessed June 2018).

4 Matthew Philips 'Art: Whitewashing Jesus'.

5 Keith Augustus Burton (2007) *The Blessings of Africa: The Bible and African Christianity*, pp. 17–18.

6 John M. Perkins, *One Blood: Parting words to the Church on race*, p. 48–9.

7 Keith Augustus Burton, *The Blessings of Africa*, p. 18.

8 Martin Meredith (2014) *The Fortunes of Africa: A 5,000 year history of wealth, greed and endeavour*, p. 40.

9 Black hermeneutics is a methodology that reappraises ancient biblical tradition and African world views, cultures and life experiences, with the purpose of correcting the effect of the cultural, ideological conditioning to which Africa and Africans have been subjected in the process of biblical interpretation.

10 Pastor Eric Mason, Pastor Jerome Gaye and Brother Berean (2017) *Slavery in the Bible: Christian history, and the white man's religion*, Frequency Conference, 24 October 2017 (available online at: <www.youtube.com/watch?v=bPT_cWaEV-Q&feature=youtu. be&app=desktop>, accessed January 2018).

11 Michael C. Burton (2008) *Deep Roots: The African/black contribution to Christianity*, p. 4.

12 Cain Hope Felder, ed. (1991) *Stony the Road We Trod: African American biblical interpretations* (Minneapolis, Michigan: Augsburg Fortress) p. 6.

13 Sheryl Sandberg Chief Operating Officer, Facebook (2017) Global Leadership Summit 2017.

14 Emma Brockes (2018) 'Daniel Kaluuya: I'm not a spokesman: No one's expected to speak for all white people', 10 February, *The Guardian* (available online at: <www.theguardian.com/film/2018/feb/10/daniel-kaluuya-not-spokesperson-black-people-black-panther-get-out>, accessed February 2018).

15 Keith Augustus Burton, *The Blessings of Africa*, p. 130.

16 Michael C. Burton, *Deep Roots*, p. 32.

17 Didymus the Blind, 'An unknown precursor of Louis Braille and Helen Keller', pp. 203–8 (available online at: <www.ncbi.nlm.nih.gov/pubmed/7995235>, accessed March 2019).

18 Keith Augustus Burton, *The Blessings of Africa*, p. 132.

19 Keith Augustus Burton, *The Blessings of Africa*, p. 133.

20 Richard Reddie (2007) 'Atlantic slave trade and abolition', 29 January, BBC News (available online at: <www.bbc.co.uk/religion/religions/christianity/history/slavery_1.shtml>, accessed March 2019).

21 Ed Stetzer (2014) 'What is contextualization? Presenting the gospel in culturally relevant ways', 12 October, *Christianity Today* (available online at: <www.christianitytoday.com/edstetzer/2014/october/what-is-contextualization.html>, accessed July 2018).

22 The Revd Les Isaac (9 June 2018) interviewed by Ben Lindsay.

23 Andrew Wilson (12 July 2018) interviewed by Ben Lindsay.

24 Andrew Wilson (12 July 2018) interviewed by Ben Lindsay.

25 Wayne Grudem (2018) 'Why building a border wall is a morally good action', 2 July, *Townhall* (available online at: <https://townhall.com/columnists/waynegrudem/2018/07/02/

why-building-a-border-wall-is-a-morally-good-action-n2496574>, accessed July 2018).

26 John MacArthur (2018) 'Social injustice and the gospel', 13 August, Grace to you (available online at: <www.gty.org/library/blog/ B180813#.W3FjqNKo1CI.twitter>, accessed July 2018).

27 Dr David A. Anderson (2010) *Gracism: The art of inclusion* (Downers Grove, Illinois: IVP).

28 Steve Tibbert (1 October 2018) interviewed by Ben Lindsay.

29 Noel Robinson (16 August 2018) interviewed by Ben Lindsay.

Interlude: Don't touch my hair

1 <https://medium.com/@strandbookstore/revolutionary-black-women-authors-7814c0b4bc60>, accessed March 2019.

2 Marverine Cole (2018) 'Black Girls Don't Cry', 20 July BBC Radio 4 (available online at: <www.bbc.co.uk/programmes/b0b9zfws>, accessed July 2018).

3 Johanna Derry (2018) 'Women in ministry: The next steps', 2 March, *Church Times* (available online at: <www.churchtimes. co.uk/articles/2018/2-march/features/features/women-in-ministry-the-next-steps>, accessed March 2018).

4 Temi (4 July 2018) interviewed by Ben Lindsay.

5 Jennifer (2 August 2018) interviewed by Ben Lindsay.

6 Nana Guar (5 September 2018) interviewed by Ben Lindsay.

7 Eleasah Phoenix Louis (10 April 2018) interviewed by Ben Lindsay.

8 Vivienne Neufville (23 July 2018) interviewed by Ben Lindsay.

5 Love like this

1 John M. Perkins with Karen Waddles (2018) *One Blood: Parting words to the Church on race and love* (Chicago, Illinois: Moody Publishers), pp. 75–6.

2 John M. Perkins (2018) *One Blood*, p. 46.

3 Dr Martin Luther King Jr (1967) 'Beyond Vietnam' speech.

4 Clifton Clarke (2017) 'Enough with racial "reconciliation"',
  21 August, *Christianity Today* (available online at: <www.
  christianitytoday.com/ct/2017/august-web-only/christians-
  combat-racism-theologically-charlottesville.html>, accessed
  March 2019).

5 Madeleine Davies (2013) 'We failed '60s immigrants', 25 October,
  Church Times (available online at: <www.churchtimes.co.uk/
  articles/2013/25-october/news/uk/we-failed-60s-immigrants>,
  accessed January 2018).

6 Madeleine Davies, 'We failed '60s immigrants'.

7 Madeleine Davies, 'We failed '60s immigrants'.

8 Steve Addison (2009) *Movements that Change the World: Five keys
  to spreading the gospel* (Downers Grove, Illinois: IVP) p. 34.

9 Makita Peters (2018) 'Bishop Michael Curry's Royal Wedding
  Sermon: Full text of 'The power of love', 20 May, npr (available
  online at: <www.npr.org/sections/thetwo-way/2018/05/20/
  612798691/bishop-michael-currys-royal-wedding-sermon-full-text-
  of-the-power-of-love?t=1531035249058>, accessed June 2018).

6 Kick in the door

1 <www.blackenterprise.com/video-deray-mckesson-equity-vs-
  equality-tech/>, accessed March 2019.

2 Harry Farley (2018) 'BAME clergy to receive special mentoring
  in Church of England bid to boost diversity', 19 April, *Christian
  Today*, 2018 (available online at: <www.christiantoday.com/uk/
  bame-clergy-to-receive-special-mentoring-in-church-of-england-
  bid-to-boost-diversity/128554.htm>, accessed April 2018).

3 Lucy Cooper (2003) 'Black and ethnic minority Christians lead
  London church growth', 25 July, Evangelical Alliance (available
  online at: <www.eauk.org/church/one-people-commission/stories/
  black-and-ethnic-christians-lead-london-church-growth.cfm>,
  accessed June 2018).

4 Race for opportunity (2012) 'Race at the top: A review of BAME leadership in the UK' (available online at: <https://race.bitc.org.uk/system/files/research/rfo_race_at_the_top_-_exec_summary_0.pdf>, accessed June 2018).

5 Earon James, 'Is Christianity the white man's religion?', Pass The Mic (available online at: <https://passthemic.fireside.fm/124>, accessed September 2018).

6 R. Kent Hughes (1996) *Acts: The Church afire* (Wheaton, Illinois: Crossway), p. 174.

7 <www.bbc.co.uk/sport/football/44174232>, accessed March 2019.

8 <www.bbc.co.uk/sport/football/44093990>, accessed March 2019.

9 Oliver Holt (2018) 'To suggest that Darren Moore's new job proves the system is now fair for black coaches is fallacy', 19 May, *Mail on Sunday* (available online at: <www.dailymail.co.uk/sport/football/article-5748835/amp/To-suggest-Darren-Moores-new-job-proves-fair-black-coaches-fallacy.html?__twitter_impression=true>, accessed May 2018). On 9 March 2019, Darren Moore was sacked from his job as manager of West Bromwich Albion. The team was fourth in the championship, in the play-off position, and was only nine points off automatic promotion back into the Premier League. The decision to sack Moore was greeted with widespread condemnation. This led presenter Andy Durham, who is white, to say on talkSPORT Radio, 'Nobody at West Brom could picture Darren Moore being successful because there are so few black managers in English football . . . therefore there is a subliminal, unconscious mindset that only white is successful.' (available online at: <https://twitter.com/talkSPORT/status/1105189147453673478>, accessed March 2019).

10 Noel Robinson (10 September 2018) interviewed by Ben Lindsay.

11 The Revd Les Isaac (9 June 2018) interviewed by Ben Lindsay.

12 Steve Tibbert (1 October 2018) interviewed by Ben Lindsay.

13 Edward S. Koh (2013) *Overcoming Cultural and Systemic Challenges: Exploring how minorities pastors overcome leadership challenges in majority culture congregations*, p. 5.

14 S. Koh, *Overcoming Cultural and Systemic Challenges*, p. 13.

15 Steve Tibbert (1 October 2018) interviewed by Ben Lindsay.

16 Jahaziel (8 March 2018) interviewed by Ben Lindsay.

17 Charlotte Sweeney and Fleur Bothwick (2016) *Inclusive Leadership: The definitive guide to developing and executing an impactful diversity and inclusion strategy*, p. 11.

18 Noel Robinson (10 September 2018) interviewed by Ben Lindsay.

19 *Stranger Things*, Season 2, Episode 2.

20 Earon James, 'Is Christianity the white man's religion?'

21 Harriet Sherwood (2015) 'C of E to fast-track minority ethnic clergy into senior roles', 25 December, *The Guardian* (available online at: <www.theguardian.com/world/2015/dec/25/church-of-england-fast-track-minority-ethnic-clergy-senior-roles>, accessed June 2018).

Interlude: Black (wo)man in a white world

1 Maya Angelou, in an interview in 1973 with Bill Moyers on TV programme *THIRTEEN* (available online at: <https://billmoyers.com/content/conversation-maya-angelou>, accessed April 2019).

2 The Revd Dr Kate Coleman (10 September 2018) interviewed by Ben Lindsay.

7 Jesus walks

1 Bryan Stevenson (2015) *Just Mercy: A story of justice and redemption* (Victoria: Scribe), p. 14.

2 Greater London Authority (2017) 'The London knife crime strategy' June 2017, p. 11 (available online at: <www.london.gov.uk/sites/default/files/mopac_knife_crime_strategy_june_2017.pdf>, accessed August 2018).

3 Richard S. Reddie (2009) *Black Muslims in Britain: Why are a growing number of young black people converting to Islam?*, p. 107.

4 Tressell Foodbank (2017–2018) 'End of year stats' (available online at: <www.trusselltrust.org/news-and-blog/latest-stats/end-year-stats>, accessed August 2018).

5 Justin Welby (2018) 'Is mixing faith and politics worth the risk?' 16 March, *Huffington Post* (available online at: <www.huffingtonpost.co.uk/entry/justin-welby-politics_uk_5aabed59e4b05b2217fe6f73?guccounter=1&guce_referrer=aHR0cHM6Ly93d3cuZ29vZ2xlLmNvbS88&guce_referrer_sig=AQAAAAqU8QGudYa8Qv7uUCvlz8bCbVGW14R5fHMJbUe7XeOec-NlTzlHgJLqtHxmthyq2Ut_tMhk18toXDI-sjIqPpCtkG99Po6Mkp-UYmCr1mvltH6LgycDLx4BqkA6BPZ27mPGdm-ZJPLc0_x_SCXVtTMD0stT1iXuy3heE3C1F12H>, accessed March 2018).

6 Kay Parris (2010) 'Robert Beckford Interview: Faith, films and theology', June, *Reform Magazine* (available online at: <www.reform-magazine.co.uk/2016/05/robert-beckford-interview-faith-films-and-theology/>, accessed August 2018).

7 Justin Welby, 'Is mixing faith and politics worth the risk?'.

8 Claire Taylor (2014) 'British churches and Jamaican migration: A study of religion and identities, 1948 to 1965', *Black Theology in Britain: A reader*, pp. 49–50.

9 Claire Taylor, 'British Churches and Jamaican migration'.

10 John M. Perkins, (2018) *One Blood: Parting words to the Church on race*, p. 74.

11 Charlie Dates (2018) *The Most Segregated Hour in America: Overcoming divisions to pursue MLK's vision of racial harmony*, MLK 50 Conference, April 2018 (available online at: <https://vimeo.com/263070525>, accessed August 2018).

12 <https://mobile.twitter.com/drantbradley/status/816446324929347584>, accessed January 2017.

13 <https://mobile.twitter.com/drantbradley/status/816448103075160064>, accessed January 2017.

14 <https://mobile.twitter.com/drantbradley/status/816449164749971456>, accessed January 2017.

15 <https://mobile.twitter.com/drantbradley/status/816450237883707392>, accessed January 2017.

16 Scott Todd (2014) *Hope Rising: How Christians can end extreme poverty in this generation* (Nashville, Tennessee: Thomas Nelson), quoting Chuck Colson, p. 30.

17 Giles Fraser (2017) 'After the Grenfell fire, the Church got it right where the council failed', 22 June, *The Guardian* (available online at: <www.theguardian.com/commentisfree/belief/2017/jun/22/after-the-grenfell-fire-the-church-got-it-right-where-the-council-failed>, accessed June 2017).

18 Giles Fraser, 'After the Grenfell fire, the Church got it right where the council failed'.

19 Bridie Witton (2018) 'Lewisham has highest school exclusion rate in London', *This is London*, 7 September 2018 (available online at: <www.thisislocallondon.co.uk/news/16695278.lewisham-has-highest-school-exclusion-rate-in-london/>, accessed September 2018).

20 <www.lewisham.gov.uk/mayorandcouncil/counciljobs/cypjobs/Pages/About-Lewisham.aspx>, accessed September 2018.

21 Cabinet Office (2017) 'Race disparity audit: Summary findings from the ethnicity facts and figures website, October 2017 (revised March 2018)', p. 8 (available online at: <www.ethnicity-facts-figures.service.gov.uk/static/race-disparity-audit-summary-findings.pdf>, accessed September 2018).

22 Doug Logan (2015) *On the Block: Developing a biblical picture for missional engagement*, p. 70.

8 Let's push things forward

1 <www.theguardian.com/news/2005/jan/04/guardianobituaries.haroldjackson>, accessed March 2019.

2 Afua Hirsch (2018) *Brit(ish): On race, identity and belonging*, p. 311.

3 Michelle Obama (2018) *Becoming* (London: Viking). Quote taken from 'Michelle Obama: A life in pictures' (available online at:

<www.vogue.co.uk/gallery/michelle-obama-a-life-in-pictures>, accessed November 2018).

4 'Remaining awake through a great revolution' speech, Dr Martin Luther King Jr, delivered at the National Cathedral, Washington, DC, 31 March 1968, Congressional Record, 9 April 1968 (available online at: <https://kinginstitute.stanford.edu/king-papers/publications/knock-midnight-inspiration-great-sermons-reverend-martin-luther-king-jr-10>, accessed October 2018).

5 Emma Brockes (2018) 'Daniel Kaluuya: I'm not a spokesman. No one's expected to speak for all white people', 10 February, *The Guardian* (available online at: <www.theguardian.com/film/2018/feb/10/daniel-kaluuya-not-spokesperson-black-people-black-panther-get-out>, accessed March 2019).

6 Emma Brockes 'Daniel Kaluuya'.

7 Roland G. Fryer Jr (2018) 'Reconciling results on racial differences in police shootings', May, *American Economic Review* (Papers and Proceedings) (available online at: <https://scholar.harvard.edu/fryer/publications/reconciling-results-racial-differences-police-shootings>, accessed October 2018).

8 <https://blacklivesmatter.com/about/>, accessed March 2019.

9 Lori Brandt Hale and Reegie L. Williams (2018) 'Is this a Bonhoeffer Moment?: Lessons for American Christians from the confessing Church in Germany', February, *Sojourners* (available online at: <https://sojo.net/magazine/february-2018/bonhoeffer-moment>, accessed March 2019).

10 'Woke' is a political term of African American origin that refers to a perceived awareness of issues concerning social justice and racial justice. It is derived from the African American vernacular English expression 'stay woke', the grammatical aspect relating to a continuing awareness of these issues.

11 <www.theatlantic.com/entertainment/archive/2015/06/nina-simone-and-mississippi-goddam/396923/>, accessed March 2019.